► *Spinner porpoise.* FRANS LANTING

► Hanauma Bay State Underwater Park. RIC ERGENBRIGHT

HAWAII
Parklands

► *A yellow-tail wrasse also called lolo, or "lazy fish."* ED ROBINSON/TOM STACK & ASSOC.

Marnie Hagmann
Number one

Hawai'i Geographic Series staff

Publishers: Michael S. Sample,
 Bill Schneider
Editors: Marnie Hagmann, Gayle Shirley
Photo editor: Jeri Walton
Design: DD Dowden
Electronic paste-up: DD Dowden
Cartography: DD Dowden
Marketing director: Kelly Simmons
Hawai'i consultant: Willis Moore

Front cover photo

David Muench, Mānana Island and tidepools at Makapu'u Beach Park, O'ahu.

Back cover photos

Top left, Greg Vaughn, dancer at an Aloha Week celebration, Hawai'i Volcanoes National Park; bottom left, Michael S. Sample, lava flow; right, Robert J. Western, 'i'iwi feeding on *Trematolobelia sp.*

Library of Congress Number: 88-80224
ISBN 0-937959-41-3 (softcover)
ISBN 0-937959-43-X (hardcover)

Design, typesetting, and other prepress work by Falcon Press, Helena, Montana.
Printed in Korea.

Acknowledgments

Hawai'i Parklands would not have been possible without generous contributions of information and assistance from Rik Cooke; Jon Erickson and Kathy English, Hawai'i Volcanoes National Park; Larry and Shirley Hagmann; Dan Moriarty, Kīlauea Point National Wildlife Refuge; Robert Nishimoto, Division of Aquatic Resources; Dan Quinn, Division of State Parks; and Jerry Shimoda, Pu'uhonua o Hōnaunau National Historic Park.

I would also like to thank publishers Bill Schneider and Mike Sample, for their confidence and support; Steve Morehouse, for reading early drafts and encouraging me; DD Dowden, for making a beautiful book; Willis Moore, for sharing his knowledge; Deb Goodin, for compiling the directory; Gayle Shirley, for her careful editing; and Matt Pavelich and Russell B. Hill, for the finishing touches.

Marnie Hagmann

Hawai'i Geographic Society owes a debt of gratitude to Bill Schneider and Falcon Press for working the concept into a reality with this Volume One. The staff of Falcon Press, especially writer Marnie Hagmann, have proven a pleasure to work with. I would add a personal *mahalo nui loa* (thanks) to the late Dr. Wayne Gagne. We were fellow staff members of the Bernice P. Bishop Museum in Honolulu and active in Sierra Club. It was Wayne who introduced me to the Volcanoes Park backcountry and to most of the conservation issues in the islands. My personal thanks are also expressed to Barbara Nickerson, with whom I explored Haleakalā Crater, Wai'ānapanapa, and Kīpahulu on Maui, which served to focus my enthusiasm for the relevance of this book.

Willis H. Moore

About the author

Marnie Hagmann was born in Santa Monica, California, and grew up in West Los Angeles. She graduated from Stanford University and went to New York City to be in book publishing. After eight years she moved to Twin Bridges, Montana, and learned to fly fish. She now lives in Helena and works at Falcon Press. *Hawai'i Parklands* is her first book.

To Foster and Mary Jane
Susan and Dale

► *Clouds brush the barren landscape of Haleakalā Crater in Hawai'i Volcanoes National Park. More than 600,000 people annually visit this extinguished volcano on eastern Maui, walking its trails and camping among the clouds.* KEVIN SCHAFER/TOM STACK & ASSOCIATES

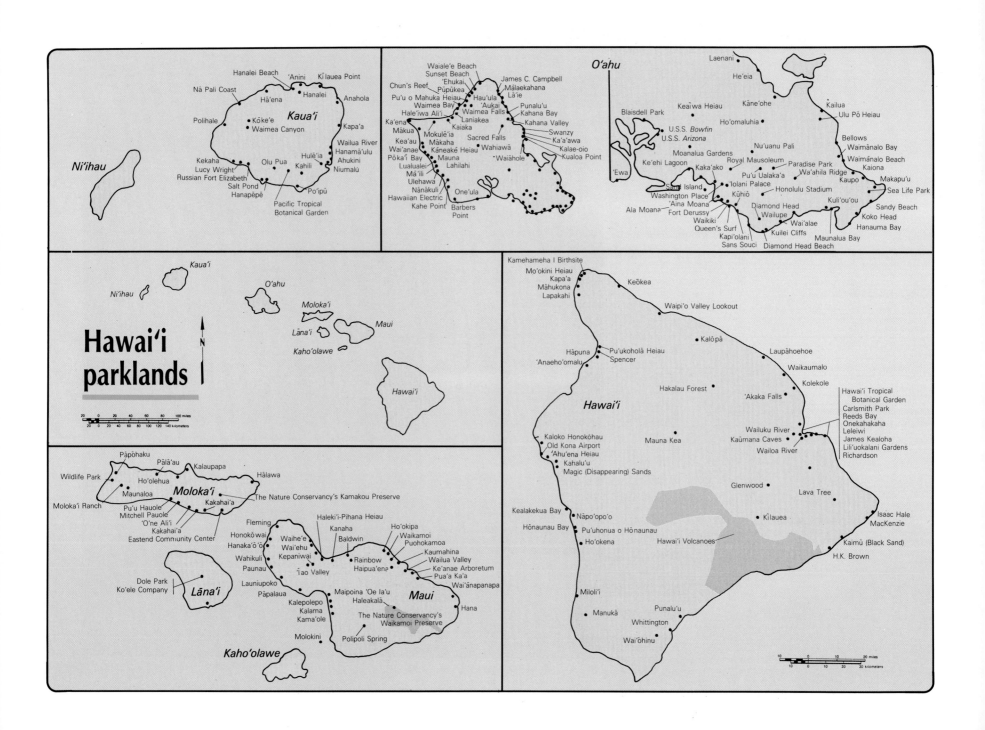

Hawai'i parklands

Ni'ihau

Kaua'i
Hanalei Beach
'Anini
Kī lauea Point
Nā Pali Coast
Hanalei
Hā'ena
Anahola
Polihale
Kōke'e
Kauai
Waimea Canyon
Kapa'a
Wailua River
Kekaha
Olu Pua
Hulē'ia
Hanamā'ulu
Lucy Wright
Kahili
Ahukini
Russian Fort Elizabeth
Niumalū
Salt Pond
Po'ipū
Hanapēpē
Pacific Tropical
Botanical Garden

O'ahu
Waiale'e Beach
Sunset Beach
'Ehukai
Chun's Reef
Pūpūkea
Pu'u o Mahuka Heiau
Waimea Falls
Hale'iwa Ali'i
Waimea Bay
Laniakea
Ka'ena
Kaiaka
Mākua
Mokulē'ia
Kea'au
Mākaha
Sacred Falls
Wai'anae
Kāneakē Heiau
Wahiawā
Pōka'ī Bay
Mauna
Lualualei
Lahilahi
Mā'ili
Waiāhole
Ulehawa
Nānākuli
Hawaiian Electric
One'ula
Kahe Point
Barbers Point
James C. Campbell
Mālaekahana
Lā'ie
Hau'ula
'Aukai
Punalu'u
Kahana Bay
Kahana Valley
Swanzy
Ka'a'awa
Kalae-oio
Kualoa Point

Laenani
He'eia
Blaisdell Park
Keaīwa Heiau
Kāne'ohe
Kailua
Ulu Pō Heiau
Ho'omaluhia
U.S.S. Bowfin
U.S.S. Arizona
Moanalua Gardens
Bellows
Nu'uanu Pali
Waimānalo Bay
Waimānalo Beach
Ke'ehi Lagoon
Royal Mausoleum
Paradise Park
Wa'ahila Ridge
Kaiona
'Ewa
Pu'u Ualaka'a
Makapu'u
Kaka'ako
'Iolani Palace
Honolulu Stadium
Sea Life Park
Sand Island
Washington Place
Kūhiō
Diamond Head
Kuli'ou'ou
'Aina Moana
Wailupe
Sandy Beach
Ala Moana
Fort Derussy
Wai'alae
Koko Head
Waikiki
Hanauma Bay
Queen's Surf
Kuilei Cliffs
Kapi'olani
Maunalua Bay
Sans Souci
Diamond Head Beach

Ni'ihau
Kaua'i
O'ahu
Moloka'i
Lāna'i
Maui
Kaho'olawe
Hawai'i

N

20 0 20 40 60 80 100 miles
20 0 20 40 60 80 100 120 140 kilometers

Moloka'i
Pāpōhaku
Pālā'au
Kalaupapa
Wildlife Park
Ho'olehua
Hālawa
Maunaloa
Moloka'i
Moloka'i Ranch
Pu'u Hauole
Kakahai'a
Mitchell Pauole
The Nature Conservancy's Kamakou Preserve
'O'ne Ali'i
Eastend Community Center

Lāna'i
Dole Park
Ko'ele Company

Maui
Haleki'i-Pihana Heiau
Fleming
Kanaha
Ho'okipa
Honokōwai
Waihe'e
Baldwin
Waikamoi
Hanaka'ō'ō
Wai'ehu
Puohokamoa
Wahikuli
Kepaniwai
Rainbow
Kaumahina
Paunau
Wailua Valley
Ke'anae Arboretum
'Īao Valley
Haipua'ena
Pua'a Ka'a
Launiupoko
Wai'ānapanapa
Pāpalaua
Maipoina 'Oe Ia'u
Kalepolepo
Haleakalā
Hana
Kalama
Kama'ole
The Nature Conservancy's
Waikamoi Preserve
Molokini
Polipoli Spring

Hawai'i
Kamehameha I Birthsite
Mo'okini Heiau
Kapa'a
Māhukona
Keōkea
Lapakahi
Waipi'o Valley Lookout
Hāpuna
Pu'ukoholā Heiau
'Anaeho'omalu
Spencer
Kalōpā
Laupāhoehoe
Hakalau Forest
Waikaumalo
Kolekole
'Akaka Falls
Hawai'i Tropical
Botanical Garden
Carlsmith Park
Reeds Bay
Wailuku River
Onekahakaha
Kaloko Honokōhau
Kaūmana Caves
Leleiwi
Old Kona Airport
James Kealoha
'Ahu'ena Heiau
Wailoa River
Lili'uokalani Gardens
Kahalu'u
Richardson
Magic (Disappearing) Sands
Mauna Kea
Glenwood
Lava Tree
Kealakekua Bay
Nāpo'opo'o
Kīlauea
Isaac Hale
Hōnaunau Bay
Pu'uhonua o Hōnaunau
MacKenzie
Ho'okena
Hawai'i Volcanoes
Kaimū (Black Sand)
H.K. Brown
Miloli'i
Manukā
Punalu'u
Whittington
Wai'ōhinu

10 0 10 20 miles
10 0 10 20 30 kilometers

Contents

► *Molten lava cascades down in a blood-red flow at Ka'ena Point at Hawai'i Volcanoes National Park.* DAVID MUENCH

Preface

You might notice that many places in Hawai'i have the same name. The ancient Hawaiians were avid namers, and they named all the features of the landscape. Since all the islands were created by the same geological processes, many of the features—and the names for them—are the same from island to island. *Waimea,* for example, means "red water," which anyone who has observed a good rainstorm in Hawai'i knows to be very descriptive. The word appears eleven times in the gazetteer of the *Atlas of Hawai'i,* three times as a town (on Hawai'i, Kaua'i, and O'ahu), twice as a bay (Kaua'i and O'ahu), and twice as a district (Ni'ihau and Kaua'i). Kaua'i has Waimea River and Waimea Canyon, O'ahu has Waimea Falls, and the Big Island (Hawai'i) has the Waimea-Kohala Airport.

Another possible source of confusion is the Hawaiian method of giving directions. You may be directed "mauka" (upward, toward the mountains) or "mākai" (downward, toward the sea). Landmarks are typically used in Hawai'i in lieu of points of the compass (Ewa direction, Diamond Head direction, windward side).

The Hawaiian language had no written form until 1829. At that time the Christian missionaries chose twelve letters to represent the Hawaiian alphabet. They picked the consonants h, k, l, m, n, p, and w; the vowels a, e, i, o, and u; and two diacritical marks, the macron, which is a straight line over a vowel (ā), and the *'uina,* or hamza, a backward apostrophe ('). The macron indicates a long, stressed vowel; the 'uina marks a glottal stop (as in, for example, the Cockney pronunciation of "bottle" as "bo'le").

The macron and 'uina are frequently omitted from written Hawaiian, but there is a growing tendency to include them. Since these marks provide helpful information about how to pronounce Hawaiian words, I have used them as much as possible.

There are few opportunities to speak Hawaiian, but pronouncing Hawaiian words correctly is very satisfying. Island people appreciate your trying to pronounce Hawaiian words correctly—they consider your efforts a gesture of respect. ■

► *The Nature Conservancy's Kamakou Preserve, which is open to the public, has been established to protect the best remaining forests on Moloka'i. This dense wall of hapu'u, 'ama'u, and uluhe ferns is near the Pepeopae bog.* DAVID MUENCH

Introduction

Mark Twain's description of Hawai'i as the "loveliest fleet of islands anchored in any ocean," coupled with the perennial reference to "Paradise of the Pacific," might lead most people to conclude that all of Hawai'i is a park—a place of beauty and a place of amusement. Some places in Hawai'i that bear the name "park" are in fact visitor-oriented places that seem to cater to the tourists rather than to preserve or interpret natural and cultural history.

For many local folk, and we do number over one million these days, the word "park" means someplace near a beach where we trek periodically for a campout or barbecue. Or the word "park" means a place in the city full of trees and open space where we can catch glimpses of blue sky or romping children.

The fact is, however, that Hawai'i parklands encompass a variety of archaeological, historic, cultural, and natural areas that are a part of Hawai'i heritage and deserve to be maintained, restored, preserved, and interpreted with loving care.

Unlike the states west of the Rockies, Hawai'i has relatively little federal land, and much of what belongs to the federal government has to do with military use. Nonetheless, the national parks and the Hawaiian and Pacific Islands national wildlife refuges encompass some areas of geologic, historic, and ecological importance. The National Park Service and the U.S. Fish and Wildlife Service have done some remarkable and unique things in the areas they administer, especially as pertains to local and cultural concerns of the Hawaiian people themselves. Sadly, however, the budget and other vicissitudes of recent years underlie a need for greater support for Hawai'i parklands on a federal level. The parks we have need more than they are getting, and the developmental needs of Kalaupapa and Kaloko Honokōhau remain largely unmet.

On the state level, the Hawai'i Department of Land and Natural Resources has a parks division and a forestry division. During its overlong apprenticeship as a territory, Hawai'i forestry and parks people often worked hard but rarely had the resources to do an adequate job. Since statehood in 1959, at neither the state level nor in the four county parks departments has there been the political or fiscal commitment to building a system of parks to be what they should be, much less to be what they could be.

Yet the challenges and opportunities are there to be met, and community resources and support are building. A growing awareness of and pride in "things Hawaiian," often called the "Hawaiian renaissance," gives impetus to preserving and interpreting places of historic and cultural significance. Some of the parks, like Lapakahi, are built around this contemporary focus. Through the diligent efforts of Sierra Club, Natural Resources Defence Council, The Nature Conservancy, National Audubon Society, and the much-older Conservation Council for Hawai'i, more awareness of and concern for Hawai'i's natural, unique, endemic, and endangered species and places are developing.

For local people, *Hawai'i Parklands* will offer a factual, interesting, informative look at the history, culture, and natural history of the islands. The lengthy narrative makes *Hawai'i Parklands* a more useful book than any of the plethora of "pretty picturebooks" which constantly wash up on the bookshelves of Hawai'i.

For the prospective resident or visitor, *Hawai'i Parklands* offers to serve as guidebook, planning advocate, and as a brief look into the history, culture, and natural history of a truly unique spot on earth. For those desiring to see and feel, to experience and absorb, what is truly special about Hawai'i, surely *Hawai'i Parklands* will prove invaluable.

Willis Henry Moore, M. Ed.
Executive Secretary and Editor
Hawai'i Geographic Society
Honolulu, Hawai'i

► *There are numerous viewpoints from O'ahu's Tantalus Drive, but Round Top in Pu'u Ualaka'a State Wayside affords one of the finest overall panoramas of the Honolulu area.* MICHAEL S. SAMPLE

Chapter one

Birth of the islands

"An eruption smells like life, like the beginning of time."

—Jon W. Erickson,
Supervisory Park Ranger,
Hawai'i Volcanoes National Park

The Hawaiian archipelago, a partly submerged mountain range, stretches 1,523 miles across the Pacific Ocean. The eight main islands—Hawai'i (the Big Island), Maui, Kaho'olawe, Lāna'i, Moloka'i, O'ahu, Kaua'i, and Ni'ihau, from youngest to oldest—are the highest peaks of the range and account for more than 99 percent of the total land area of the state, or 6,425 square miles. Northwest of Ni'ihau, 124 tiny islands, reefs, and shoals—the eroded remnants of older mountains—extend as far as Kure Atoll, the western boundary of Hawai'i. At Kure, the chain angles north to join the Emperor Seamounts, an even older submerged range that runs almost to the Soviet Union's Kamchatka Peninsula.

Scientists believe that each of these islands, all volcanoes, was fueled by a fixed hot spot in the earth's mantle under the Pacific Plate. Each was built of countless layers of lava from innumerable volcanic eruptions. The hot spot, a permanent source of magma (lava beneath the surface of the earth), is stationary, while the Pacific Plate overrides it at the rate of one to three inches every year. The plate moves in a northwesterly direction, carrying the islands with it. This movement stretches an island's volcanic plumbing,

decreasing the frequency of eruptions until the volcano is considered dormant. Finally, the plumbing breaks, rendering the volcano extinct. But over the hot spot itself, a new volcano starts to grow on the sea floor.

The Pacific Plate's northwesterly journey terminates in the Aleutian Trench, where the edge of the plate, islands and all, is subducted under the northern plates and remelted in the earth's mantle.

Meanwhile, erosion attacks the islands as they emerge from the ocean. Driving rains, battering waves, and powerful winds all sculpt dramatic landforms out of the once-symmetrical volcanoes. Eventually, they wear the islands down to sea level. The crust sags under their sheer weight, and the islands gradually sink beneath the waves and continue drifting northwest as submerged seamounts.

Evidence of these geologic processes appears throughout Hawai'i, but the parks preserve some of the best examples. From the new lava flows at Hawai'i Volcanoes National Park to the spectacular eroded landscape of Kaua'i's Nā Pali Coast State Park to the tiny atolls of the Hawaiian Islands National Wildlife Refuge, Hawai'i's parklands tell a fascinating geologic life story

Hawai'i Volcanoes National Park

Five separate volcanoes—Kohala, Hualālai, Mauna Kea, Mauna Loa, and Kīlauea—make up the Big Island, the youngest and largest island in the chain.

► Pāhoehoe from Kīlauea, Hawai'i's most active volcano, has added seventy-five acres of new land to the Big Island since 1986. The surface of a pāhoehoe flow cools first, insulating the lava underneath. As a result, the lava can run for many miles.
MICHAEL S. SAMPLE

► *A steamy sulphur vent, left, adds to the inhospitable landscape surrounding Kīlauea's summit caldera.* D. CAVAGNARO

► *'Ama'uma'u, right, is a pioneer of new lava flows. This species of fern is found only in the Hawaiian islands.* GREG VAUGHN

Hawai'i Volcanoes National Park, at 229,000 acres, covers portions of Mauna Loa and Kīlauea, the only active volcanoes in the state. The fact of their eruptions means they are still on top of the hot spot.

Mauna Loa, "Long Mountain," began forming three million years ago. Magma from the earth's mantle welled up out of the hot spot and puddled as lava on the sea floor, 18,000 feet beneath the surface. Under the water's enormous pressure, these upwellings accumulated in innumerable thin layers until, after two million years, the volcano broke the surface. In less than a million years, frequent eruptions of hot, fluid lava—the latest was in 1984—brought the mountain from sea level to its height of 13,677 feet.

In profile, Mauna Loa's gradual slopes resemble an immense warrior's shield lying face up on the ground. It shares this characteristic with other Hawaiian volcanoes and explains why they are known as "shield" volcanoes. For visitors who are used to a level horizon, the Big Island's slant takes some getting used to. On the older islands, erosion has mostly

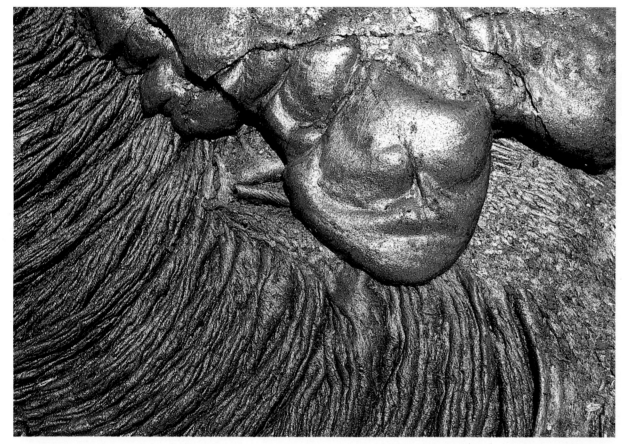

► *Swirling, billowing textures characterize pāhoehoe lava, one of the two main types of lava produced by Hawaiian volcanoes. The other is thick, rough ʻaʻā.* D. CAVAGNARO

► *Related to huckleberries, blueberries, and cranberries, ʻōhelo berries can be eaten raw or cooked into pies or preserves. The berries are considered sacred to Pele, the volcano goddess, and Hawaiians always offered a branch of the berries to Pele before eating any themselves.* GREG VAUGHN

obliterated the original shield-like shape.

Kīlauea, at 4,093 feet, is the smallest and most active Big Island volcano. It has the distinction of being the current home of Pele, the traditionally tempestuous Hawaiian fire goddess. She is said to live in Halemaʻumaʻu Crater, a secondary fire pit in the Kīlauea summit caldera. To guard against aging, Pele keeps this part of the island looking geologically young with regular applications of new lava. In fact, Kīlauea has erupted continuously since January 3, 1983.

Bountiful though her lava may be, Pele is deeply possessive of it. According to contemporary mythology (but with no basis in Hawaiian tradition), park visitors who take lava samples home as souvenirs will later suffer bad luck and misfortune. They can usually end their troubles by sending the rocks back to the park. A showcase in the visitor center displays rocks that have been returned with respectful, apologetic notes.

Hawaiian lavas, among the hottest on earth, are of two types: *pāhoehoe* (pronounced pa-hoy-hoy) and *ʻaʻā* (as you

would say ah-ah to a misbehaving child). Hot, fluid pāhoehoe lava has a smooth, swirling surface texture that results from uneven cooling. The lava next to the ground stays hot and liquid, while the surface cools and stiffens. The texture comes from the still-plastic crust being dragged along by the hotter lava underneath, which can flow at relatively high speeds. As pāhoehoe cools and loses its gas content, it can turn into 'a'ā, a rough, viscous, slow-moving, and crumbly type of lava. When it cools, 'a'ā is hard and durable. Some flows begin and continue as 'a'ā. Although Hawaiian lavas come from the same source, their characteristics can vary from flow to flow. Some flows, for example, resist erosion better than others.

Although relatively mild-mannered compared with volcanoes such as Washington's Mount St. Helens, shield volcanoes put on a good show. In fact, Mauna Loa's and Kīlauea's awe-inspiring pyrotechnical displays draw thousands of spectators. True volcano fans will hop on a plane at a moment's notice to observe phenomena such as "curtains of fire" (when lava issues in sheets from newly opened fissures) and 2,000-foot-high lava fountains. The park provides up-to-date eruption information via a twenty-four-hour recorded message at (808) 967-7977.

▶ *Lava spews from a rift zone in a "curtain of fire" on Kīlauea's flank. The volcano has been known to erupt for years at a time, although not with this intensity.* KEN SAKAMOTO

Many people believe that a geothermal explanation does not adequately describe the incredible power of an eruption. It's the spiritual force of Pele, they say. Where once they propitiated her with branches of sacred 'ōhelo berries, Pele's followers now favor her with bottles of gin and other offerings. The thought of harnessing Pele's power for electricity, a plan which is being considered for a site outside the park, is deeply repugnant to many Hawaiians.

Having Pele on your side can make a big difference. In 1790 a band of warriors en route to battle marched across Kīlauea. They were killed in an explosive surge of incandescent ash, giving their opponent, the great chief Kamehameha, a tremendous psychological advantage in his campaign to unify the islands. Their footprints in the Ka'ū Desert are still visible. To see them, take the paved, 3.6-mile Mauna Iki trail, which starts 9.1 miles southwest of park headquarters on Highway 11.

Other volcanic artifacts at Hawai'i Volcanoes include tree casts and molds. When a lava flow invades a forest, the trees resist burning long enough for the lava to harden around their trunks and preserve their shape. Then they ignite, sometimes burning for weeks until no organic trace remains. If the flow recedes from the forest, it leaves behind a coating of lava on the trees. These cylindrical casts, known as "lava trees," indicate the depth of the flow. There are lava trees near Kīlauea and at Lava Tree State Monument on Highway 132 southeast of Pāhoa, about fifteen miles from the park.

If the lava does not recede, the tubular impressions left by the trunks are called tree molds. You can see examples off the Mauna Loa Road. Pāhoehoe at the right temperature and viscosity takes a very fine impression, preserving minute details of the wood.

In places where pāhoehoe has been confined to a channel, the cooling surface of the flow forms an insulating crust, permitting the lava to run freely underneath, sometimes over great distances, until it is stopped by the sea or by the end of the eruption. The resulting lava tubes were used as shelters or burial caves by early Hawaiians and were sometimes decorated with petroglyphs (carvings in the rock). The lighted, 400-foot Thurston lava tube, an unusually large example set in a tree-fern jungle off Crater Rim Drive, was discovered in 1913 by local newspaper publisher and conservationist Lorrin Thurston.

When lava explodes into the air in the absence of water, as in a fountain, volcano products such as Pele's hair and Pele's tears are sometimes created. Pele's tears, rounded lumps of volcanic glass, are very common in Hawai'i, and Pele's hair, which is volcanic glass spun into strands by a blast of gas, can be found as well.

When lava cools so rapidly that the gas bubbles in it don't burst, it creates pumice. Light and airy, pumice seems harmless, but it was a blanket of pumice cinders that killed the forest on the Devastation Trail near Kīlauea.

The fascinating study of Hawaiian volcanoes brought pioneering volcanologist

► *The unusual formations in Lava Trees State Park date back to 1790. In that year Kīlauea erupted, discharging more than thirty-seven million cubic yards of lava. Some of the lava flooded a grove of 'ōhi'a lehua trees at the present site of the park. The lava destroyed the grove but left behind casts of the trees.*
DAVID MUENCH

► '*Ōhi'a lehua saplings, left, reclaim a pāhoehoe flow at Hawai'i Volcanoes National Park. Endemic to Hawai'i, the 'ōhi'a's small seeds are easily dispersed by the wind—one reason why it is among the first plants to pioneer new lavas.*
BEVERLY MAGLEY

► *Like stars in a midnight sky, seashells sparkle against the black, volcanic sand of Kamoamoa Beach, right, at Hawai'i Volcanoes National Park.* LARRY ULRICH

Thomas A. Jaggar to the islands earlier this century. Acting on the belief that an understanding of the workings of volcanoes would reduce loss of life and property, he set up the Hawaiian Volcano Observatory in 1912. Scientists at the observatory continuously monitor seismic and volcanic activity, gathering information with sensitive instruments such as seismographs and tiltmeters. Seismographs register the swarms of minor earthquakes that usually precede an eruption and indicate the underground movement of magma. Tiltmeters measure the "swelling" of the volcanoes prior to eruption.

Administered by the U.S. Geological

Survey, the observatory shares Crater Rim Drive, the park's most traveled road, with the Thomas A. Jaggar Museum, where you can find the answer to almost any question concerning volcanoes; the Kīlauea Visitor Center, where a short film orients visitors to the features of the park; the Volcano House hotel, where the restaurant serves pie made from Pele's favorite 'ōhelo berries; and the Volcano Art Center, where a fine gallery features the work of local artists and craftsmen.

Kaimū Beach

When the ocean stops the progress of a lava flow, the contact of molten lava with cold seawater generates steam. The lava explodes into millions of tiny fragments, forming an instant, romantic black sand beach. Picturesque Kaimū Beach, a county park four miles east of Hawai'i Volcanoes on Highway 130, is a famous example. Wai'ānapanapa State Park on Maui has a small one, and there are others scattered throughout the islands. Unfortunately, black sand beaches tend to disappear, washed away by the waves, sometimes in a matter of days. But this only adds to their mystique.

Waipi'o Valley Lookout

When a volcano is tall enough to trap clouds, it catches moisture from the northeasterly trade winds. The water runs down the slopes of the volcano's shield in ever-deepening channels, carving V-shaped gulches, steep-sided canyons, ridges as sharp and narrow as knife blades, and broad, flat-bottomed valleys.

The windward side of the mountain, the side facing into violent winter storms, erodes faster. The lee side, protected by the volcano's rain shadow, stays drier and remains relatively unscarred. In time the mountains wear down until they no longer create effective rain shadows, and the dramatic effects of erosion are distributed more evenly from one side of the island to the other, as on Moloka'i, O'ahu, and Kaua'i.

Kohala, the oldest volcano on the Big Island, is situated on the wet, windward northern tip of the island. Inactive for 60,000 years and dissected with high, near-vertical cliffs and deep, sloping valleys, the volcano has become a mountain range—the fate of exposed volcanoes on Maui, Moloka'i and O'ahu. On O'ahu, for example, the Ko'olau Range, once a single volcano, has been worn into a narrow ridge.

The island of Kaua'i is deeply dissected but has retained a flat summit plateau with an elevation higher than the summits of the younger islands O'ahu, Moloka'i, and Lāna'i. The caldera of the main volcano, like Kīlauea's Halema'uma'u only much bigger, filled with lavas that hardened into caprock. These lavas have resisted erosion so that at 5,243 feet, Kaua'i's Kawaikini is the eighth-tallest mountain in Hawai'i. On its windward side is one of the wettest places on earth, 5,148-foot Mount Wai'ale'ale, which receives an average of 450 inches of rain a year.

At Waipi'o Valley Lookout, a county

► *Waipi'o Valley in the Kohala Mountains at the northern end of the Big Island is a result of water erosion. The wide, flat-bottomed valley, usually viewed from Waipi'o Valley Lookout at the mouth of the valley, is ideal for taro farming. A four-wheel-drive road is the only access.* GREG VAUGHN

► Cinder cones, silverswords, and other plants adapted to extreme conditions share the cloud-filled crater of Maui's Haleakalā. DAVID MUENCH

park fifty miles north of Hilo, you can observe the effects of relatively early stages of erosion. Standing on the shoulder of a more recent lava flow from Mauna Kea, you can look down into a great flat-floored chasm cut into the Kohala Mountains. This formation, called an amphitheater-headed valley, also occurs in Honolulu at Mānoa Valley (home of the University of Hawai'i), which you can observe from Wa'ahila Ridge State Recreation Area or from Roundtop (elevation 1,048 feet) in Pu'u Ualaka'a State Wayside. Hālawa Valley near Hālawa Park on the eastern tip of Moloka'i is another example.

Diamond Head State Monument

Diamond Head, Hawai'i's most famous landmark, is a tuff cone, a type of volcanic formation particularly common on O'ahu. When lava comes into contact with water, steam explosions are generated that tear the lava into tiny fragments known as ash. The ash piles up around the vent to become a cone, and the material is eventually cemented into the soft rock called tuff. Other tuff cones on O'ahu are Punchbowl Crater, site of the National Memorial Cemetery of the Pacific; Koko Head and Koko Crater in Koko Head Regional Park; the bay in Hanauma Bay State Underwater Park; and Ulupa'u Head at Kāne'ohe Marine Corps Air Station.

Climbers may be attracted to tuff cones, but any attempt to climb the unstable rock can result in injury. However, at Diamond Head State Monument in Honolulu, you can picnic in a landscaped meadow on the crater floor and climb up the trail 760 feet to the rim for a panoramic view of the city and the Kāhala plain.

Haleakalā National Park

A prime example of a volcano in various stages of erosion, Maui's Haleakalā was set aside as a national park in 1916. Geologists believe that the mountain's spectacular summit crater was not the result of volcanic cataclysm but of stream erosion.

Two streams cut V-shaped gulches into the 12,000-foot volcano. The gulches grew into amphitheater-headed valleys that eventually met at the summit. This meeting created a long, erosional slash that looks like a crater. When the volcano erupted again, lava poured down the stream valleys, nearly filling them and creating the effect of a crater rim. Further activity added crunchy cinders, symmetrical cinder cones, ash, spatter (formed by the combination of gas and liquid lava), volcanic bombs (large lumps of spatter), and other products.

Haleakalā is quiet now, so quiet that the clouds billow almost audibly over its barren, lunar-like crater. The mountain is 10,023 feet tall with a crater depression 3,000 feet deep, 7.5 miles long, and 2.5 miles wide. The tallest cinder cone, Pu'u o Maui, stands 500 feet above the floor. Visitors who arrive in time to watch the sun rise over the eastern rim say it's an unforgettable sight. Whether they're responding to the actual sunrise or the crowd of spectators, some wrapped in blankets, some dressed as if for space flight (they will ride bicycles back down the mountain), is hard to say.

Geologists consider the volcano dormant but not extinct. Its latest activity occurred in 1790, with two minor flows along the southwest rift zone near La Perouse Bay. As Maui, second-youngest island in the chain, drifts to the northwest, the possibility of Haleakalā's erupting again becomes increasingly remote.

'Iao Valley State Monument

Two volcanoes, Haleakalā and the older West Maui volcano, formed the island of Maui. Near Wailuku in the foothills of the West Maui Mountains, velvety green 'Iao Needle is the handiwork of erosion. The 1,200-foot prominence was once part of a ridge on the West Maui volcano. Valleys ate into the ridge from either side, creating a saddle. Eventually the saddle wore away, leaving only the needle, a free-standing volcanic sculpture.

The centerpiece of 'Iao Valley State Monument, 'Iao Needle is a volcanic plug, dike, or throat. Lava caught in this throat after the last eruption was denser and less susceptible to erosion. The most dramatic example of such a plug is Mount Olomana on O'ahu, which stands 1,643 feet above sea level.

Waimea Canyon State Park

Kaua'i's Waimea River, aided by faulting, has created a masterful work of erosion in Waimea Canyon State Park. At one time rainwater drained off the central dome of Kaua'i in symmetrically radiating streams. Then a series of downthrusts altered the topography of western Kaua'i, creating a depression parallel to the west coast. This depression diverted west-side watercourses into the south-flowing Waimea River. Its erosional force resulted in Waimea Canyon, the yawning, red gorge aptly called the "Grand Canyon of the Pacific."

► In the West Maui Mountains, erosion-resistant 'Iao Needle, a lava neck, was left behind when water wore away the ridge that once connected it to the neighboring peak. DOUGLAS PEEBLES

► *The Waimea River has carved a "Grand Canyon of the Pacific" out of the layers of lava that constitute the island of Kaua'i. For those not satisfied with the view from the overlooks, hiking trails lead into Waimea Canyon State Park.* DAVID MUENCH

► *Clouds and mist soften the sharp points and contours of the Kalalau Valley in Nā Pali Coast State Park. Kaua'i's advanced age, more than five million years, is most evident in these deeply eroded formations.*
ED COOPER

Nā Pali Coast State Park

Whether you view the famous Nā Pali coastline from a motorized raft, a sightseeing helicopter or airplane, or on foot via the Kalalau Trail, you have to remind yourself that, like the other islands, Kaua'i began as a gently sloping shield volcano. Five million years of exposure to wind, rain, and surf has given Nā Pali Coast State Park a landscape like no other—knife-edged ridges, deep, round-headed valleys, precipitous cliffs from 300 to 2,000 feet high, sea caves swirling with surf.

Runoff of Kaua'i's extravagant rainfall hones the ridges and carves out the valleys, but waves create the cliffs and the scenic coastline. When waves hammer at the volcanic shield, parts of it give way to form dramatic cliffs, or pali. (Nu'uanu Pali State Wayside on O'ahu provides a spectacular view of the pali on that island's windward side.) Waves cutting into a layer of less-resistant lava lying under a more-resistant layer cause the formation of sea caves, natural arches, and spouting blowholes. Or the overhanging layers may simply collapse, leaving more cliffs.

The trail into this exciting, rugged world, eleven miles one way and frequently slippery from rain, is part of a circumisland footpath constructed hundreds of years ago by the Hawaiians. Improved only slightly during the WPA, the trail begins at Hā'ena State Park at the end of Highway 56 near Hā'ena.

▶ *Anemone-like tube coral secretes a stony skeleton, which is covered by a thin layer of living, vibrantly pigmented tissue.*

ED ROBINSON/TOM STACK & ASSOCIATES

Hā'ena State Park

Adjacent to the Nā Pali Coast, Hā'ena State Park illustrates the difference a protective coral reef can make to an island's coastline. The gentle character of the beach here, with its beautiful white sand and protected swimming, quickly changes to dramatic, wave-pounded sea cliffs where the reef stops.

As coral reefs weather, the ocean washes particles of coral onto the shore, where they accumulate in luxurious deposits of sand. Reef formation takes millions of years, especially in these relatively cool Hawaiian waters. On the older islands, particularly Kaua'i and O'ahu, white sand beaches have had time to develop. The Big Island, by contrast, has very few beaches.

Another feature of Hā'ena State Park is its former sea caves. The ancient caves were formed by wave erosion at a time when the ocean was higher. Perhaps anticipating plate tectonics, Pele once took them for a home but then abandoned them for warmer digs closer to the hot spot.

Hawaiian Islands National Wildlife Refuge

Older than Kaua'i—but privately owned and closed to the public—is Ni'ihau, "the Forbidden Island." Beyond Ni'ihau, which is the last major island of the archipelago, lie the Northwestern Hawaiian Islands. These tiny islands, remnants of mountains worn down to nubbins, consist perhaps of a beach, a lagoon, and a ring of coral. In 1906 President Theodore Roosevelt established the Hawaiian Islands National Wildlife Refuge to protect these islands and their wildlife and native plants. The environment is so delicate that permission to land on any of the islands must be obtained from federal and state regulatory agencies.

Eventually, these sandy atolls, reefs, and shoals will subside completely under the waves and drift into the Aleutian Trench. But the pattern of island life—birth by emergence from the waves, growth by eruption into a massive shield, decay by erosion, death by drowning, and disposal by subduction—has been repeated for millions of years. In fact, the newest addition to the chain, Lo'ihi Seamount, a submarine volcano about thirty miles southeast of the Big Island, lies just 3,300 feet beneath the surface. It will be thousands of years yet, but Lo'ihi may someday break the surface to form the next island in the Hawaiian chain. ■

► *The sandy beaches of the Hawaiian Islands National Wildlife Refuge at the northwestern end of the archipelago are prime habitat for Hawaiian monk seals. The species is related to tropical seals in the Caribbean and the Mediterranean. At the turn of the century, monk seals were nearly extinct. Now, despite protection, their numbers are declining due to human disturbance, shark predation, and disease. Except for the Hawaiian bat, the Hawaiian monk seal is the only mammal native to Hawai'i.* D. CAVAGNARO

The life of the land

"Nowhere is there a better opportunity to catch nature at work than in Hawai'i."

—Hampton L. Carlson,
professor of genetics,
University of Hawai'i

Hawai'i was not always a lush, tropical paradise. When the oldest islands were new, some ten million years ago, they were bleak and inhospitable. No raucous mynas greeted the dawn. No ginger, pikake, or plumeria perfumed the air. No kiawe thorns pierced sandals. No monstera vines tangled the forests. No coconut palms graced the beaches. There was nothing but barren lava.

Scientists speculate that the first plants came to Hawai'i as seeds carried by birds in their feathers, in their digestive tracts, and in the mud on their feet. Saltwater-resistant seeds washed up on the beaches after storms. Floating mats of vegetation carried other plant seeds, along with snails and other small creatures. Lightweight seeds, fern spores, spiders, and small insects drifted there on the wind. Birds and sturdy insects such as dragonflies and butterflies flew or were blown in by storms. It may sound as though lifeforms swarmed onto the islands, but the establishment of new species was actually quite rare. A new plant appeared perhaps once in a hundred thousand years, a new bird once in a million years.

An estimated 250 plants, fifteen land birds, 250 insects, some twenty land mollusks, and two mammals made the trip to Hawai'i, successfully established themselves, and, except for the mammals (the Hawaiian bat and the Hawaiian monk seal), evolved into thousands of new species not found anywhere else on earth. These plants and animals are known as "endemic" species, meaning that they occur naturally only in the islands of Hawai'i.

Evolving for millions of years in an essentially closed system, isolated by 2,000 miles of ocean from the nearest continent, endemic species adapted in unique and unusual ways to their environment. For example, mint plants lost their pungent oils, raspberries their thorns, some birds and insects the ability to fly. A caterpillar became carnivorous.

Hawai'i was a world of birds, insects, land snails, and plants. In such a land, without grazing animals, many species lost any aggressive tendencies and their ability to compete. Endemic species became extraordinarily vulnerable to outside influences.

This fragile Hawaiian world began to change about 1,500 years ago when the first humans—the Polynesians—arrived. They found a few familiar plants, some strange flightless birds such as the three-foot giant owl, ibis, and goose, and not much to eat except fish.

But the Polynesians came prepared to pioneer the new lands. They brought with them the plants, cuttings, and seeds they would need to grow food, medicine, fiber, and building material. These utilitarian plants included yams, sweet potatoes, taro, bananas, sugarcane, coconut palms, breadfruit, and others—about two dozen species in all. The Polynesians also brought jungle fowl, or moa, and small pigs and dogs used for food and sacrifice. Stowaways—rats, mice, skinks, geckoes, and many kinds of weeds and insects—made the crossing as well.

From an ecological point of view, these settlers had an enormous impact on the islands. The early Hawaiians used fire to clear the native forest so that they could cultivate the land, diverted streams for irrigation, terraced the hillsides, made fish ponds from coastal mudflats, and hunted some birds to extinction. They irrevocably altered the landscape, especially at the lower elevations. Descendents of their pigs and jungle fowl roam the islands, and the plants have thrived, sometimes crowding out endemic species.

The rate of change accelerated dramatically after 1778, when Captain James Cook made his first Hawaiian landfall. Since then, people have brought plants and animals—and their diseases—from all over the world. Finding rich volcanic soil, abundant rainfall, and an equable climate, they have made Hawai'i the lush, tropical paradise it is today. Unfortunately, introduced species prey on or compete with endemic plants and animals, which have no defenses against the new threats.

Hawai'i's endemic species are a precious legacy. Scientists study them to better understand evolution and ecology. Students of nature find them a source of wonder, tourists a novelty. To the people of Hawai'i they are an important responsibility, and to all Americans they represent a part of our natural heritage as surely as the redwoods of California or the grizzlies of Montana.

► 'Ōhi'a lehua blossoms around an old snag in Kīlauea Iki crater in Hawai'i Volcanoes National Park. The trees have regrown since the last lava flow here in 1959. D. CAVAGNARO

But sugarcane and pineapple cultivation, logging, cattle ranching, and now real estate development all threaten endemic species. Many have become extinct, and many more will doubtless be lost.

Many of Hawai'i's parklands try to preserve endemic species and remnants of the original vegetation, but they are disappearing fast. Some parks display landscapes restored to pre-Cook conditions, providing ethnobotanical insight into early Hawaiian culture. And parks throughout the islands offer intriguing glimpses of exotic plants and animals from all over the world.

Hawai'i Volcanoes National Park

► Unlike most geese, the nēnē, or Hawaiian goose, lives far from water on sparsely vegetated slopes in Hawai'i Volcanoes and Haleakalā national parks. Endemic to Hawai'i, the nēnē is the state bird. GREG VAUGHN

Hawai'i Volcanoes National Park offers much more than volcanoes. It embraces several life zones, from the barren lava fields of the Ka'ū Desert to the tree-fern jungle along Crater Rim Road. It protects a wide range of endemic species and contains interesting examples of the evolutionary phenomenon of *kīpuka*.

Where lava flows cover the ground, small patches of land sometimes remain untouched. These pockets of fertile soil, known as kīpuka, are surrounded by lava that may not support life for hundreds of years. A few of the plants and animals that survive within the kīpuka may evolve eventually into unique species. As a result, some Hawaiian species have a worldwide distribution of only a few acres.

Kīpuka Puaulu, or Bird Park, off Mauna Loa Road is a good example. Fenced in by younger lava flows bearing only scrubby vegetation, the hundred-acre kīpuka supports a lush native forest, including magnificent koa trees, forest patriarchs one hundred feet tall and up to six feet in diameter. Sometimes mistaken for eucalyptus trees by casual observers, koas are a type of acacia. Their leaves are sickle-shaped *phyllodes,* or flattened leaf stems. They produce small yellow flowers, which mature into flat, brown seed pods up to six inches long and an inch wide. The wood is as highly prized by woodworkers today as it was by early Hawaiians, who made canoes, surfboards, paddles, house timbers, and bowls and containers from koa.

Another conspicuous tree of the kīpuka—one widely distributed throughout the state—is the 'ōhi'a lehua. Like many native plants in Hawai'i, it assumes a variety of forms, depending upon where it grows. Here it grows up to eighty feet tall with a diameter of more than four feet. Outside the kīpuka, on dry lava flows, it may be only a ten-foot-tall shrub. Along with several varieties of aggressive ferns, it is among the first plants to pioneer new lava flows. It dominates the wettest forests, and in mountain bogs it grows as a dwarf shrub less than a foot tall. This member of the myrtle family has extremely small seeds, easily borne on the wind, which may explain how it came to Hawai'i and how it has found so many habitats. With dark green foliage, dark grey bark, and gnarled, twisted branches, 'ōhi'a trees lend an air of solemnity to the forest, but this mood is dispelled as soon as they flower into a riot of vivid red blossoms. 'Ōhi'a wood—dark red, heavy, and very hard—has some commercial value.

Signs along the 1.2-mile, self-guided nature trail through open meadows and deep forest point out the native Hawaiian plants in Kīpuka Puaulu. You might also see native forest birds such as the crimson-and-black, nectar-eating 'apapane feeding on 'ōhi'a blossoms or the rare, bright-yellow, endangered 'akiapōla-'au, hammering on a koa. (The upper mandible of this bird's bill is long, curves downward, and is useful for probing in bark, while the lower mandible is stout and wood-peckerlike. To feed, it throws its upper bill back and pounds furiously with the lower, then digs for insect larvae with the upper.)

There is nowhere else on earth like Kīpuka Puaulu, and the National Park Service works hard to keep it that way by fencing out destructive wild pigs and removing nonnative vegetation. Twelve to fifteen "special ecological areas" have been designated in the park to preserve native species and their original habitat, but this kīpuka is the easiest to visit.

The park is also home to upland birds, such as the native nēnē, the state bird of

► An 'i'iwi feeds on Trematolobelia sp. *The plumage of this endemic forest bird was used extensively in Hawaiian featherwork.* ROBERT J. WESTERN

Hawai'i. A type of goose, the endangered nēnē measures twenty-two to twenty-six inches long, has lost most of the webbing between its toes, and lives on rugged, sparsely vegetated volcanic slopes, far from water. Through modestly successful breeding programs, it has been reintroduced to Haleakalā National Park on Maui. Approximately a thousand birds exist in the wild, but predators such as the mongoose keep their numbers depressed.

Famous in India as a cobra killer, the mongoose was introduced in 1883 to eradicate rats and mice in sugarcane fields. (Hawai'i's only snake, the harmless, termite-eating blind snake, is thought to have come to O'ahu from the Philippines in 1929.) Unfortunately, the sleek, brown, ferretlike animal has had a greater impact on ground-nesting birds than on rodents.

The Hawaiian hawk, or 'io, another endangered native, soars gracefully on thermals rising from the heated lava beds, but the Hawaiian crow, or 'alalā, is nearly extinct. More visible are Kalij pheasants, introduced game birds, which frequently dart out of the forest onto the road. Males are a metallic bluish black with white barring on their backs and grey breasts. Females are mottled brown, and both sexes have crests.

Haleakalā National Park

▶ *This shapely young silversword along the Sliding Sands Trail of Maui's Haleakalā will grow as many as twenty years before producing a single stalk of flowers. The plant's compact shape and silver-haired leaves protect it from the intense sunlight and help it conserve moisture.* MARNIE HAGMANN

From the 250 progenitor plant species that originally found their way to Hawai'i, scientists estimate 2,500 new species evolved. One of those ancestor plants was a type of sunflower, and it has branched out into a group of twenty-eight related plants known as the silversword alliance. The most famous member of the group, the Haleakalā silversword, grows exclusively in Haleakalā National Park.

This remarkable plant has adapted to a high-elevation environment between 7,000 and 10,000 feet, where it must contend with intense sunlight, low humidity, and widely fluctuating temperatures. Its long, spiky leaves, silver-haired to deflect the sun and conserve moisture, swirl in a striking rosette pattern. With its compact round shape, measuring about two feet in diameter, it bears no obvious physical resemblance to a sunflower. It lives between five and twenty years, and flowers once, usually beginning in May. It produces a single stalk, three to eight feet tall, of 100 to 500 yellow or reddish purple flowerets. After the seeds mature, usually by October, the plant dies.

At one time silverswords were so abundant in Haleakalā that people uprooted them and rolled them down the slopes of the crater for sport. The plants were also harvested and dried and sent to the Orient, where they were used for decorative purposes. Vandalism and predation by goats and insects caused an alarming decline in their population, and by 1927 only a hundred plants were left in the crater. The National Park Service instituted conservation programs, and the species has made a comeback. A fence around the entire crater now keeps out feral goats, but two new invaders, the Argentine ant and the Vespula wasp, potentially threaten the silversword.

Other members of the silversword alliance include the Ka'ū silversword found on the southwest rift zone of Mauna Loa in Hawai'i Volcanoes National Park. A single lava flow could wipe out the entire population. The related greensword, now rare, lacks silver hairs and grows in the rain forests and bogs on the windward slopes of Haleakalā.

A world away from the silversword-and-cinder landscape of Haleakalā crater is the park's Kīpahulu district, a three-hour, sixty-two-mile drive from Kahului via the Hana Highway. Added to the park in 1969 to protect rare native birds and plants, most of the area is a scientific research reserve closed to the public. You can, however, visit scenic 'Ohe'o (pronounced o-hay-o) gulch, swim in the lovely pools, hike up the gulch two miles through a bamboo forest to Waimoku Falls, picnic, camp, and generally enjoy one of the values preserved here—*ho'o-nānea,* meaning to pass the time in ease, peace, and pleasure.

'Ohe'o Gulch is sometimes mistakenly referred to as "the Seven Sacred Pools," when actually there are more than twenty pools in the first mile of 'Ohe'o Stream above the ocean. These pools contain rare native Hawaiian freshwater fish, shrimp, and snails. Descendants of marine forms, they lead a precarious life in streams that can become raging torrents in a matter of minutes. 'Ohe'o Stream has been known to rise four feet in ten minutes.

One stream resident, the *'o'opu,* a type of goby, breeds and lives its adult life in the upper stream. But when its eggs hatch, the current sweeps the microscopic larvae downstream to the sea. Weeks later, the tiny 'o'opu fry return to the stream mouth and begin an amazing journey back up the waterfalls and terraces to their adult habitat. Their pelvic fins have fused into a strong suction disk that enables them to climb up the waterfalls by alternately clinging tightly with their fins and squirming forward with their tails. 'O'opu fry have been observed climbing a smooth vertical surface at the rate of eighteen inches in twenty seconds and hanging upside down on the undercut rock faces of waterfalls.

Like most coastal areas in the islands, 'Ohe'o Gulch shows the effects of human intervention, both by ancient Hawaiians and more recent inhabitants. Most of the plants in the forest here were introduced, including Java plum, native to the East Indies and Burma; christmasberry, native to Brazil; mango, native to India; and tropical almond, native to the East Indies. Cane grass, six feet tall and native to Africa, lines the path next to the parking area. In season, rotting guavas litter the trails and highway.

Guava, native to tropical America, was brought to Hawai'i about 1800 and cultivated for use in jelly, juice drinks, and other products. When it escaped from cultivation, the fast-growing plant became a serious pest throughout the islands. A twenty-to-thirty-foot-tall tree in wet forests or a six-to-ten-foot-tall shrub in exposed areas, it crowds out native plants. Wild pigs, birds, and people eat

▶ *The pale green foliage of kukui trees is easy to spot in the Kīpahulu district of Haleakalā National Park. Mist from lower Palikea Falls catches the sun to make a rainbow, while Waimoku Falls spins a silvery thread in the background. The Waimoku Falls Trail follows 'Ohe'o Gulch to the base of the waterfall.* ED COOPER

► *A fence keeps feral goats, left, out of the crater, but goats still inhabit other parts of Haleakalā National Park. These healthy animals were spotted on Kalapawili Ridge.* PHILIP ROSENBERG

► *Rooting about the forest floor, feral pigs, right, disturb native vegetation and create openings that introduced plants will fill.* GREG VAUGHN

the round yellow fruits, widely dispersing the seeds.

Wild pigs pose a grave threat to the Kīpahulu district, the scientific reserve, and sensitive areas on all the major islands except Lānaʻi. A cross between the small pig of the Polynesians and the large European variety, they often weigh more than 200 pounds and sometimes as much as 400 pounds. Rooting through the delicate ferns and mosses of the forest floor, they destroy countless rare plants, create openings for exotic plants, distribute plant seeds in their droppings, and contribute to the spread of diseases, such as avian malaria. (Their rooting makes depressions that trap water where mosquitoes—not native to Hawaiʻi and vectors of malaria—can breed. Native Hawaiian birds are extremely vulnerable to avian malaria.)

Fences keep some areas pig-free, and hunting helps control their numbers. In the rain forests, where the largest populations occur, they are often hunted with dogs. Some sportsmen use only a long knife to dispatch the pig while their dogs hang on to its ears and snout. Pigs taken from drier habitat are said to be better eating than those from the wet forests, but in any case, more hunting of pigs will help preserve vital native habitat.

Wailua Valley State Wayside

The route to 'Ohe'o Gulch follows the narrow, thin-shouldered, winding Hana Highway along the scenic northern coast of Maui. Several waysides provide relief from the road. One of them is Wailua Valley State Wayside, thirty-two miles, or 2.25 hours, east of Kahului airport.

Here a staircase climbs up through a dense tangle of hau trees to a scenic overlook. Hau occurs naturally in Hawai'i and in other tropical coastal areas, probably because its seeds float. The tree has low, spreading branches, broad, leathery, heart-shaped leaves, and abundant flowers, which turn from yellow to orange to red during the course of a day. As you're walking through the thicket, you can imagine early Hawaiians looking for matching pairs of the crooked limbs. They used them to make the struts attaching the outrigger to the hull of their outrigger canoes. Light but strong, the wood was also used for adze handles and fishnet floats; the fibrous bark for twine, rope, net bags, sandals, and a coarse grade of kapa cloth. A soft block of hau and a sharp stick of a hard wood were used to make fire.

From the top of the stairs, the view looks inland to the Ke'anae Valley and misty Ko'olau Gap in the rim of Haleakalā. The Nature Conservancy's Waikamoi Preserve, open to the public by appointment, is located on these steep rain-forested slopes. The preserve

► *Waterfalls along the scenic Hana Highway, some with swimmable plunge pools at their bases, tempt travelers to abandon the winding road.* JAMES RANDKLEV

▶ *Waterbirds such as the endangered Hawaiian coot, or 'alae-ke'oke'o, face habitat loss and pressure from predators.* BRIAN PARKER/TOM STACK & ASSOCIATES

protects the last realm of the Maui creeper and crested honeycreeper, two members of an intriguing family of land birds that, like Darwin's famous Galapagos finches, share one common ancestor. Surpassing Darwin's finches, which diversified into only twelve or so species and subspecies, the Hawaiian honeycreepers diversified into at least thirty-seven.

The palest green patches of foliage on the lower slopes of Haleakalā are kukui trees. This Polynesian import, a member of the spurge family, grows in moist lowland forests as well as in gorges and gulches in dry regions. The kukui was named the state tree of Hawai'i because, as the law states, "the multiplicity of its uses to the ancient Hawaiians for light, fuel, medicine, dye, and ornament and its continued value to the people of modern Hawai'i, as well as the distinctive beauty of its light green foliage which embellishes many of the slopes of our beloved mountains, causes the kukui tree to be especially treasured by the people of the Fiftieth State of the United States."

Raw kukui nuts are a powerful laxative, but roasting them removes the toxicity.

Pounded and mixed with salt and chili pepper, they make a condiment called *inamona*. Nuts were once squeezed for oil to burn in stone lamps and strung on the midribs of coconut leaves to burn as candles. Then as now they are polished and strung in attractive leis. Dyes were extracted from the husks and shells of the nuts, the bark, and the roots. Gum from kukui trees strengthened kapa cloth and preserved fishnets.

In the other direction from the scenic overlook, toward the ocean, lie the peaceful farms and taro patches of Wailua Valley. From earliest times, Hawaiians have cultivated taro. They cook and eat the leaves like spinach and use them to wrap the meat and fish served at a luau. Poi, the starchy staple of their diet, comes from the roots. Fortunately for waterbirds, Hawaiians still relish poi. Taro farms provide almost the only wetland habitat left for four endemic, endangered waterbird species: the Hawaiian coot (*'alae-ke'oke'o*), Hawaiian stilt *(ae'o)*, Hawaiian gallinule (common moorhen or *'alae'ula*), and Hawaiian duck *(koloa maoli)*.

Wai'ānapanapa State Park

Three hours (52.8 miles) from Kahului and ten miles before 'Ohe'o Gulch, Wai'ānapanapa State Park makes a fine destination. This remote, wild, 120-acre park has a low-cliffed volcanic coastline, a small black sand beach, a seabird colony, cave pools, a native hala forest, sea stacks, a natural stone arch, blowholes, and a *heiau* (place of worship). Other attractions include camping, shore fishing, and hiking along an ancient Hawaiian coastal trail into Hana, approximately three miles away. Cabins furnished with many amenities are available to rent.

The hala grove at Wai'ānapanapa is one of the largest remaining in Hawai'i. Indigenous to the Pacific islands and parts of Asia, the hala is also called pandanus or, in Australia, screwpine. It occurs naturally in Hawai'i (its seeds float) at elevations from sea level to 2,000 feet. The Polynesians brought along their own cultivated varieties.

Hala trees are either male or female. Both have stiltlike aerial roots and three-to-six-foot-long narrow, flexible leaves. But females bear fruit and males have fragrant flowers, called *hinano*. The wood of female halas is hard on the outside but soft inside, and early Hawaiians used hollowed-out branches as water pipes. The wood of male trees is hard throughout and was used for serving or storage bowls, canoe rollers, and house posts.

In addition to the wood, the Polynesians used every part of the tree. The leaves, or *lauhala,* normally have spines along the edges and the midribs, which the Polynesians stripped off before weaving the material into thatch, sails, floor coverings, sleeping mats, room partitions, and many household items. The silky white bracts of the male flowers were woven into very fine mats used only by Hawaiian chiefs and priests. The pollen from the male flowers was believed to be an aphrodisiac, and it was also used as a preservative for feather leis and kahilis (feathered standards that were the symbol of royalty). Oil from the bracts was a headache remedy, and the flowers relieved constipation.

► *A sea stack covered with beach naupaka at Wai'ānapanapa State Park provides a safe nesting area for seabirds. Atop the low volcanic cliffs is one of the largest groves of hala trees in the islands.* DAVID MUENCH

▶ *Heliconia blossoms, like hanging lobster claws, are a colorful, exotic surprise in wet forest areas.* PHILIP ROSENBERG

The individual fruits, called "keys," are wedge-shaped and grow in compact clusters of fifty or more. They are about the size and shape of pineapples and turn yellow, orange, or red as they ripen. Ripe keys fall from the cluster, littering hiking trails and filling the air with a pleasant perfume. The narrow, inner end of the key is edible, with a flavor and texture between beeswax and sugar cane. Evidently, the fruit had little appeal for early Hawaiians, as other cultures developed tastier varieties elsewhere in the Pacific. The inner ends of unripe keys are still strung with ferns to make fragrant lei. Dried, the fibrous keys were once used to apply dye to kapa cloth. Even the aerial roots were used to make hula skirts. Red-footed boobies nest in the tops of these twenty-foot trees.

Some hala groves had names perpetuated in Hawaiian songs and legends and were celebrated for their fragrance. Groves have been lost due to tidal waves and fires, and many have been cleared for housing construction and farming. But the tree is popular with landscapers, and its future seems guaranteed.

Beach naupaka is a common coastal shrub at Wai'ānapanapa and in tropical areas throughout the Pacific Basin. Its seeds, encased in buoyant, round, fleshy white berries about half an inch in diameter, still germinate after spending extended periods in saltwater—an efficient means of dispersal.

Beach naupaka provides cover for ground-nesting seabirds such as the wedge-tailed shearwater, but don't expect to see such birds here. Most seabirds have moved to offshore sea stacks and islets, like the colony of noddies near the black sand beach, where predators—mongooses, rats, dogs, and cats—can't reach their nests.

Another attraction of Wai'ānapanapa are the caves. To reach them, leave the old Hawaiian footpath at the black sand beach and follow the signs a short distance inland. The trail leads through a hala-and-hau jungle, a grassy area, and a tunnel of hau to the caves and their crystal-clear pools. Framed by lush ferns, ti, yellow ginger, and impatiens in pink, coral, and white, the pools might be a trysting place for lovers. But according to Hawaiian legend, the spot has had a violent history. At certain times of the year, the pools appear to be stained red, supposedly by the blood of a Maui princess who was slain there. In fact, the red color comes from periodic hatches of tiny freshwater shrimp, about the size and shape of mosquito wrigglers.

Nā Pali Coast State Park

Kaua'i's Nā Pali Coast is an area of unsurpassed beauty. Because of its cliffs and relative inaccessibility, developers have left it alone. Until this century, the area supported a sizeable Hawaiian population. Now it is a 6,175-acre state park, frequented by backpackers and wild goats.

Settling here as early as 1200, Hawaiians terraced the valleys and established fishing villages along the beaches. Via a narrow footpath, they traveled between the lush valleys of this region. Hikers can follow this footpath, called the Kalalau Trail, from the trailhead at Ke'e Beach in Hā'ena State Park eleven miles to the Kalalau Valley.

The first few miles through coastal forest fragrant with hala and overripe guava can be treacherous, with tree roots, stream crossings, lava boulders, and slippery mud to impede your progress. The climate becomes progressively drier as you go southward, from the windward to the leeward side of the island.

Exotic vegetation abounds on the Nā Pali Coast, due partly to the Hawaiian presence and to the cattle ranch that once operated there. Pungent, thorny lantana, with its colorful clusters of pink, orange, yellow, white, red, or lavender flowers, is one of the most troublesome plants. Brought to Hawai'i in 1858 as a garden shrub, it has become a severe problem, despite efforts to eradicate it.

A less strenuous way to appreciate this remote wilderness park is by motorized raft, helicopter, or airplane. You can also enjoy a good view of the Kalalau Valley from overlooks at Kōke'e State Park.

▶ *The red-footed booby is commonly found throughout the tropical Pacific. Immature birds are a dull brown, and develop white plumage over the first three years.* MIKE BOYLAN

Kīlauea Point National Wildlife Refuge

► *The green sea turtle, or* honu, *now a federally protected species, is becoming more common in Hawaiian waters.*
FRANS LANTING

Modern Hawaiian mythology has it that the two breeding pairs of mongooses brought to Kaua'i for rodent control were swept off the dock by a chance wave and drowned. Whether or not the story is true, no mongooses live on the island, making it a safer place for birds. And at no place are birds safer than at Kīlauea Point National Wildlife Refuge, off Highway 56 on the north side of Kaua'i.

Kīlauea Point offers an excellent opportunity to observe seabirds in restored native habitat. A picturesque lighthouse was built here in 1913 to guide trans-Pacific shipping fleets through the islands and was placed on the National Register of Historic Places in 1979. In March 1988 the refuge acquired 1.25 miles of pristine shoreline, from Crater Hill out to Mōkōlea Point. Visitors can explore the new lands by taking a three-hour docent-led hike.

The U.S. Fish and Wildlife Service became interested in Kīlauea in 1974 because it held one of the most productive seabird colonies in the major islands. Since then the service has replanted hundreds of hala trees and beach naupaka shrubs to improve the habitat for red-footed boobies and wedge-tailed shearwaters. Other re-established native plants include 'u-lei, pohinahina, 'ilima, 'akoko, pā'u-o-hi'-aka, and 'āheahea.

Unlike other Hawaiian boobies, the red-footed variety builds a crude nest off the ground in a shrub or tree. With red feet and legs, a blue bill, a forty-inch wingspan, white feathers, and black wingtips, these birds are common throughout the tropical Pacific.

Wedge-tailed shearwaters are important fish locators for fishermen, who watch where they gather to feed. Skimming close to the surface of the water and then "shearing" into the waves, shearwaters catch fish and squid that have been driven to the surface by schools of tuna. Their webbed feet make it possible for them to kick off from the crest of a wave, and they can stay at sea for months without coming to land. Located at the base of their beaks, these birds have a "tube nose," which protects their nostrils from ocean spray and is connected to a gland that removes extra salt from their diet. Since they build their nests in burrows, people can accidentally crush them underfoot, and they are easy prey for predators. At the refuge their burrows are safe among beach naupaka shrubs, fenced off from predators and pedestrians.

Other bird species that use the refuge include the Laysan albatross, great frigate-bird, red- and white-tailed tropic birds,

Pacific golden plover, Newell's shearwater, ruddy turnstone, and brown booby.

The Hawaiian green sea turtle is sometimes seen in these waters, foraging on seaweed. Adults weigh from 200 to 500 pounds, have carapaces ranging from two to four feet long, and are olive tan in color (the green in the name refers to the color of their fat). Although preyed on by tiger sharks and hunted by early Hawaiians as a favored offering to the gods, the species held its own until the 1950s and 1960s. Then restaurant demand for the meat and tourist demand for tortoiseshell souvenirs made turtles commercially attractive, and the population plummeted. Now they are protected as an endangered species.

The humpback whale, forty-five feet long and weighing up to forty-five tons, is an annual visitor here from December to April. A baleen whale, the humpback strains seawater through its comblike strips of baleen to extract herring, plankton, and krill. Migrating from Alaska, the whales winter in these warm waters where they mate and give birth.

Whale calves are born tail first, weigh one ton, and measure fourteen feet in length. At birth, the mother quickly nudges her calf up to the surface so that it can learn to breathe and swim. It drinks rich mother's milk for the first eleven months and will grow to twenty-five feet in the first four months. Look for whales here and off Poʻipū on the other side of the island; in the channel between Molokaʻi, Lānaʻi, and Maui; off the Kona Coast and South Point on the Big Island; and near Hanauma Bay on Oʻahu.

► *This Laysan albatross chick at Kīlauea Point National Wildlife Refuge will have a wing span of eighty inches when it grows up.* GREG VAUGHN

▶ *Hawaiians have used koali, a type of morning glory, for a variety of medicinal purposes.* D. CAVAGNARO

Polihale State Park

Across the island from Kīlauea Point lies Polihale State Park, the westernmost point on Kaua'i and the westernmost park in the United States. As you travel there, you may be surprised to hear the flutelike song of the western meadowlark, which was introduced to Kaua'i from the mainland in 1931. You'll also see cattle egrets prowling in the pastures for insects and other tidbits. These conspicuous white birds were introduced to the islands from Florida in 1959 for pest control. Now they are something of a nuisance. As you head west on Highway 50 and enter the island's rain shadow, the vegetation thins out and the climate changes, becoming hot and dry.

A five-mile-long, dusty, red dirt road continues where the highway stops, winding through dull green cane fields. Sugarcane came to Hawai'i with the Polynesians, but it was not until the nineteenth century that sugarcane cultivation became a profitable business. In the days before much thought was given to ecology, the planters brought in a variety of animals to help protect their crops.

One such animal was the mongoose. Another was the giant neotropical toad, which was introduced from Puerto Rico in 1932 to eat sugarcane beetles and other insects. "Giant" refers to the fact that females, the larger of the sexes, grow six to eight inches long. Common on all the main islands in gardens as well as cane fields, you might see roadkilled specimens, as big as dinner plates and just as flat.

The cane fields give way to a broad sandy beach backed by sand dunes. Behind the dunes rise low hills covered with koa haole and scrubby kiawe trees, a type of mesquite native to South America. Kiawe was introduced in 1829 by the Catholic missionary Father Bachelot, and it has proved a mixed blessing. Although the tree provides shade in hot, arid locales, its long thorns are a menace. Its leaning, branching shape recalls the cypresses of Monterey, but its deep root system depletes the groundwater.

Koa haole, or "foreign koa," is an imported species, as the name implies. Called "koa" because its leaves resemble those of true koa seedlings, it was introduced early in the nineteenth century as cattle fodder and has spread aggressively in dry areas throughout the islands.

The sand dunes at this beach park are among the largest in the state. Anchored by sprawling morning glory vines and other low-lying plants, this dune complex displays an unusual variety of native flora. Patterns of human habitation and land use usually dictate that shoreline areas receive the brunt of the impact. None of this, however, will have any affect on the vivid sunset or the excellent view of Ni'ihau across the channel. Walk to the end of the beach and scramble over the water-worn lava boulders on the spit to get a real sense of land's end.

Ka'ena Point State Park

Land's end on O'ahu is at Ka'ena Point State Park. Like Polihale, it is situated on the westernmost point of the island, features a similar hot, dry climate, and has sparse vegetation. Located at the end of Farrington Highway (Highway 930), Ka'ena Point is approachable from either the north or the leeward shore. Beyond its broad sandy beach, tidepools teem with marine life. Here, too, are small wave-cut natural arches, excellent views, and scattered examples of native Hawaiian cotton, or *ma'o*.

Once much more widespread, this member of the hibiscus family has been displaced by kiawe and koa haole. In old Hawai'i, the bright yellow flowers yielded a yellow dye, and the leaves and bark a green dye, unusual in Polynesia. Healers prescribed an infusion of the flowers and other plant parts for stomach complaints. Today ma'o has a role in agriculture. The fibers in the bolls are too short for textile use, but the plant is more insect-resistent than commercial cotton. Ma'o is related closely enough to the commercial strains to be interbred, potentially cutting the costs of cotton production.

► *The slipper lobster, or* ula papapa, *can be found on the walls of caves or on shallow reef flats at night—or on restaurant menus.*
ED ROBINSON/TOM STACK & ASSOCIATES

► *It resembles a barnyard chicken, but this jungle fowl, or moa, at Kōke'e State Park is descended from the fowl the Polynesians originally brought to the islands.* ROBERT J. WESTERN

Kōke'e State Park

Located about thirty miles from Polihale State Park and at 3,600 feet elevation on the upper plateau of Kaua'i, Kōke'e State Park seems far removed from the hot beaches and arid foothills below. A forested area with a cool, pleasant climate, 4,345-acre Kōke'e adjoins Waimea Canyon State Park and offers many attractions, including camping, picnicking, viewing the spectacular Kalalau Valley on the Nā Pali Coast, hiking, fishing for rainbow trout, birding, maile gathering (maile is the fragrant, hard-to-find vine used to make lei for important occasions), and exploring the margins of the intriguing Alaka'i Swamp. The park, one of the most frequently visited in the state, also offers lodging in well-equipped cabins.

Kōke'e and the surrounding forest reserves provide important habitat for native forest birds. Indeed, the remote and relatively inaccessible Alaka'i Swamp, which borders Kōke'e, is the last stand for some of Hawai'i's rarest birds, such as the Kaua'i 'ō'ō, whose yellow thigh feathers decorated the capes and helmets of ancient chiefs; the Kaua'i 'akialoa, with its long curved bill; kāma'o, a type of Hawaiian thrush; puaiohi, or small Kaua'i thrush; 'ō'ū, a yellow-and-green Hawaiian honeycreeper; and nuku-pu'u, another rare honeycreeper.

One trail to the Alaka'i Swamp starts at the end of the paved road past the Kalalau lookout. A short stretch of dirt road, an aborted road-building effort, leads into a damp forest of twisted, moss-covered 'ōhi'a trees and ferns. Depending on the cloud cover, you may or may not realize you are walking along a ridge with breathtaking views of the waterfalls and great fluted cliffs of the Kalalau Valley to the west. Skinks rustle in the leaf litter at your feet. These small, slim lizards were probably stowaways aboard Polynesian canoes. Four species are found in Hawai'i. The metallic skink, the most common, is a coppery tea color, has smooth, shiny scales, and eats insects.

Along the path grow fluffy lichens, combinations of algae and fungi. Elsewhere lichens play an important role in soil formation, breaking down bare rock surfaces to develop pockets of soil that permit progressively larger plants to grow. In Hawai'i, lichens colonize new lava flows, but they are most abundant in wet, foggy regions such as this one. Flowering plants, such as 'ōhi'a trees, often appear before lichens on new lavas.

Farther into the red claylike mud of the Alaka'i Swamp, the 'ōhi'a trees become smaller. Deep in the bog, individual trees may be only a foot tall. 'Ōhi'a forms aerial roots on its trunk, and some older trees bear tangles of branches where 'ōhi'a seedlings and other plants can take root, contributing to the jungly atmosphere of the swamp.

► *At the edge of the Alaka'i Swamp bordering Kōke'e State Park on Kaua'i, the lush vegetation includes tree ferns and gnarled 'ōhi'a lehua.* ED COOPER

Kōke'e offers many other hiking trails and opportunities to enjoy spectacular scenery that might be preferable to an expedition into the indelible red mud of the swamp. Jungle fowl, descendants of those brought by the Polynesians, strut like barnyard chickens around the natural history museum and lodge. Seen throughout the islands, Pacific golden plover, or *kōlea* (the Hawaiian word for "boastful"), abound in the fall and winter months. Around the first of May, they leave Hawai'i in flocks and head for their nesting grounds on the Alaskan and Siberian tundra 2,000 miles away.

Introduced plants, especially blackberries and banana poka, a stringy vine with hanging pink flowers, are choking out much of the native vegetation. The spread of these pests is partly due to hikers, who carry the seeds from place to place on mud-encrusted boots.

Polipoli Spring State Recreation Area

Located on the southwestern slopes of Haleakalā in the Kula Forest Reserve on Maui, ten-acre Polipoli Spring State Recreation Area is an example of an almost completely exotic forest, very different from the forests of Kōke'e.

By the turn of the century, native forests had declined greatly due to uncontrolled livestock grazing, fires, cutting for firewood, clearing for farming, and invasion by introduced insects, diseases, and plants. Planters, cattlemen, and other residents recognized the urgent need to protect the watershed (forests keep rainwater from running off into the ocean) and reestablished cover on denuded forest areas.

Under the direction of Ralph S. Hosmer, who served as the first territorial forester from 1904 to 1914, hundreds of species of trees were brought to Hawai'i from all over the world. Exotics were thought to be faster growing, more commercially valuable, and better able to take and hold the land than native species. Some had no value for forest products but made a dense, persistent cover. Others had value for ornamentation, wood, windbreaks, fruit, or erosion control. The trees used included redwood, Monterey cypress, sugi, ash, tropical ash, Mexican pine, red alder, Port Orford cedar, eucalyptus, swamp mahogany, and blackwood.

The result of reforestation at Polipoli Spring is a forest of great beauty—mysterious, dark, deep, and very quiet.

Despite the steep dirt road with its many switchbacks and poor visibility, Polipoli Spring is well worth visiting. Miles of hiking trails wind through the fog belt of Haleakalā, among stands of fragrant redwood and less familiar trees. The understory of delicate ferns and mosses (torn up in places by wild pigs) adds to the enchantment. Fruit trees abound (Methley plums ripen betweeen May and July). You can hunt wild pigs and upland birds, such as California quail, ring-necked pheasant, and chukar (a type of partridge) in season. The camping area, in a deeply shaded clearing at 6,200 feet elevation, might be unexpectedly damp and cool (in winter, nighttime temperatures are frequently below freezing), so bring extra clothing.

'Akaka Falls State Park

In 1923, the Territory of Hawai'i set aside sixty-five acres near Hilo as a territorial park. As plans for the park progressed, plants from all over the world were brought to this rainy spot on the Big Island. The result is a lush, tropical rain forest with two beautiful waterfalls fifteen miles north of Hilo.

'Akaka Falls, which became a state park in 1960, features a paved .4-mile loop trail that takes off from the parking area under the branches of a huge tree. Follow the trail counterclockwise into the canyon to first visit 100-foot Kahuna Falls and then 420-foot 'Akaka Falls. These falls, both on Kolekole Stream, are most dramatic during wet weather when the river is at its highest. The trail passes two smaller falls, fifteen and eighteen feet high, on a smaller stream, and climbs back to the parking lot.

The moss-covered trail (be careful, it's slippery) descends into a tangled, confusing world of green. Familiar hala trees, the ubiquitous 'ōhi'a, complicated banyans, banana trees, stands of bamboo, and tree ferns are festooned with a massive growth of spreading monstera, its aerial roots hanging like curtains from the trees. Ti, coffee, thimbleberries, and selaginella ferns add more shades of green. For color accents (this is only a partial list) there are orchids in the branches overhead, impatiens in varying shades of pink and salmon, lazily hanging heliconia blossoms, bird of paradise, begonias, flowering plumeria trees, bougainvillea, morning glory, hibiscus, azaleas, and ginger—giant Fijian, torch, and shell.

Ironically, very few of the plants here are native, yet this is what many expect Hawai'i to look like, the Hawai'i of travel posters.

► *'Akaka Falls State Park near Hilo features four waterfalls. The tallest, 'Akaka Falls, left, on Kolekole Stream, drops 420 feet.* GREG VAUGHN

► *In 1923 the hibiscus, top right, was named the flower of the territory of Hawai'i. Now it is the state flower and an indelible trademark of the islands.* DOUGLAS PEEBLES

► *Widespread, fragrant, and attractive, Plumeria, or frangipani, bottom right, is commonly used in making lei.* JOHN J. SMITH

'Iolani Palace State Park

► *A white, or fairy, tern incubates its single egg on the branch of an ironwood tree. This snow-white seabird's wide-eyed look is created by the black ring around its dark blue eye.* D. CAVAGNARO

Cities are ecosystems, too, and the beautifully landscaped grounds of 'Iolani Palace in downtown Honolulu are a good place to observe the urban environment. The trees here are the kinds found in big cities in tropical areas throughout the world, but they may be unfamiliar to visitors from the mainland: umbrella-shaped monkeypods, a banyan that could easily accommodate the Swiss Family Robinson, noni (Indian mulberry), kapok, false kamani (Indian almond), and hala.

Many species of urban birds frequent the palace grounds, including the common myna, zebra dove, spotted dove, house sparrow, house finch, white tern, Pacific golden plover, warbling silverbill, nutmeg mannikin, chestnut mannikin, red-vented bulbul, red-whiskered bulbul, northern cardinal, red-crested cardinal, Java sparrow, and one native bird, the 'amakihi.

These birds were brought to Hawai'i for reasons ranging from scientific to sentimental. The common myna, for example, was introduced from India in 1866 to control army worms and cutworms, which were destroying sugarcane fields and pastures. A loud, aggressive bird, it congregates in large flocks in the evenings to roost in banyan or monkeypod trees. It begins vocalizing before dawn, doing nothing to enhance its popularity. Although useful in devouring insects of all kinds, it also

► *Popular as potted plants in the nineteenth century, banyans from India found their way to many locales in the islands. This climbing banyan, or strangler fig* (Ficus sp.), *is at O'ahu's Waimea Falls Park arboretum.* MICHAEL S. SAMPLE

damages crops, spreads weeds and mites, and interferes with the nests of native birds. On the lawn at the palace, it displays its unusual ability to walk as well as hop.

Compared with the ungainly pigeons common in mainland cities, zebra doves and spotted doves, both introduced from Asia, are attractive alternatives. The familiar house, or English, sparrow was released on O'ahu in 1871, and the house finch was introduced from California in 1870. The warbling silverbill, from Asia, was first seen on O'ahu in 1984. Mannikins came from southeast Asia, the nutmeg in 1865 and the chestnut between 1936 and 1941. The bulbul population resulted from an unauthorized cage release in the 1960s. The northern

cardinal came from the eastern United States in 1929, and the red-crested cardinal from South America in 1928. The Java sparrow is an escaped cage bird.

Urban birds contribute to the control of weeds, insects, and biodegradable litter. But they can also be a health hazard, spreading parasites, adding to noise pollution, and interfering with airplane traffic. But by developing an interest in accessible urban birds, people may come to appreciate less familiar (and more threatened) birds.

The impact on Hawai'i of the ancient Polynesians, of the nineteenth-century planters and ranchers, and of present-day real-estate developers has been enormous. Yet pockets of native habitat, beleaguered

and frayed, remain. If the H.M.S. *Beagle* had stopped at the Hawaiian Islands instead of the Galápagos, Darwin would have alerted the world a hundred years sooner to the fabulous evolutionary heritage of Hawai'i. Instead, man came late to this realization and has had to institute dramatic measures to slow (but not halt) the loss of habitat, of species, of genetic diversity. By setting aside parklands, The Nature Conservancy, the National Park Service, the State Department of Land and Natural Resources, the U.S. Fish and Wildlife Service, the Trust for Public Land, and other agencies are working to preserve Hawai'i's legacy for the future. In the meantime, Hawai'i has much to offer the casual and the trained observer. ■

Chapter three

The Hawaiians

In approximately A.D. 500, Polynesians from the Marquesas Islands came to Hawai'i, crossing more than 2,000 miles of the Pacific Ocean in double-hulled voyaging canoes. They navigated by the stars and read the sky and the ocean to chart their course.

Settling first at South Point, the southern tip of the Big Island, their population grew from fewer than 100 to an estimated 300,000 by the time of Captain Cook's first contact in 1778. Between 1200 and 1300 Hawai'i was invaded by a taller, stronger race of Polynesians from Tahiti. With new vitality infused into their culture, the Hawaiians briefly extended their colonization to the tiny island of Nihoa far to the northwest.

Skilled fishermen, the Hawaiians used nets, spears, traps, and hooks to harvest food from the ocean. Resourceful farmers, they used fire to clear the land for cultivation, terraced the hillsides, and built irrigation systems. Traces of their work are barely visible, but the results—coconut palm beaches, pale green kukui groves, spreading breadfruit trees—are widespread. Early aquaculturists, they made stone-walled fish ponds for the husbanding of mullet fish. Most of the fish ponds have disappeared, but a few have survived and remain commercially viable.

These early Hawaiians also brought the gods from their southern homelands: Kū, Kāne, Lono, and Kanaloa. Kū, god of war, was also invoked for rain, growth, fishing, and sorcery. Kāne, *primus inter pares,* was god of sunlight, forests, and fresh water and was the progenitor of all humans—chiefs and commoners. Thunder, clouds, wind, the sea, agriculture, and fertility were the province of Lono, who could assume as many as fifty forms. Kanaloa was the god of healing and lord of the ocean and its winds. Lesser and more specialized deities included Pele, the volcano goddess, and Laka, patron goddess of hula dancers. Maui was the famous demigod who forced the sun to slow down on its course through the heavens to make the days longer. Divining what the gods meant by their actions and appeasing them was the job of a highly skilled expert, the *kahuna.*

The Hawaiians worshipped these and many more deities in an open-air temple called a *heiau* (pronounced "hay-ow"). With a few exceptions, the structures have been reduced to amorphous piles of lava rocks. Brooding and enigmatic, whether reconstructed or left as rubble, heiau are a powerful—and the most visible—reminder of the ancient Hawaiian presence, and some are preserved in the state's parks.

Hawaiian life began changing with the arrival of Captain Cook in 1778 and the subsequent waves of European and American visitors and settlers. In 1819, after the death of Hawai'i's greatest chief, Kamehameha I, sweeping social and religious changes obliterated much of the past. However, in institutions such as the Bernice P. Bishop Museum in Honolulu, in national parks and monuments such as Pu'uhonua o Hōnaunau on the Big Island, in numerous state and county parks, and in private hands, Hawai'i's cultural heritage is being preserved and interpreted for generations to come.

► Coconut palms cast early morning shadows across A-frame structures, or halau, and a traditional outrigger canoe, carved from koa wood, on the palace grounds at Pu'uhonua o Hōnaunau. JEFF GNASS

Pu'uhonua o Hōnaunau
National Historical Park

Hawaiians were governed by chiefs, or *ali'i,* who were considered one level below the gods. Their *mana,* or spiritual power, was so great that commoners had to lie down on the ground—or be instantly executed—whenever ali'i were near. Anything an ali'i touched was imbued with his power, became immediately sacred, and was from that moment his personal possession. Even the shadow of an ali'i was charged with mana and could not be touched on pain of death. These *kapu,* or taboos, strengthened the ali'i's connection to the divine.

In addition to the regulations surrounding the person of the ali'i, there were dietary kapu forbidding women to eat certain foods, such as pork, coconuts, bananas, and shark meat, and forbidding men and women from eating with each other. Kapu seasons were established that prohibited the gathering of some foods at specific times of the year. When these kapu seasons coincided, for example, with the breeding cycles of fish, they acted as conservation measures, much

▶ Ki'i *grimace protectively at the entrance to* Hale o Keawe *in Pu'uhonua o Hōnaunau. Offerings were placed on the* lele, *the raised platform in the background.* DAVID MUENCH

like modern fishing regulations. Chiefs or priests could also declare kapu for arbitrary reasons.

To break a kapu was to offend the gods, and the Hawaiians believed the gods reacted violently to such insults by bringing tidal waves, famines, lava flows, or earthquakes down upon them. Kapu-breakers were pursued, captured, and put to death by stoning, clubbing, or strangulation or by being burned or buried alive. The penalty was the same no matter what kapu was broken.

Fortunately for kapu-breakers, they could take refuge in a sanctuary, or *pu'uhonua*. Pu'uhonua were imbued with powerful mana by virtue of the bones of ali'i interred in their temples. If a kapu-breaker eluded his pursuers and reached a pu'uhonua, his life was spared. The priest in charge of the sanctuary performed an absolution ceremony, and in a few hours or days the kapu-breaker could safely go home. Others who found refuge in a pu'uhonua were defeated warriors and those too old, too young, or unable to fight.

Considered overwhelmingly sacred because of the long line of chiefs—the ancestors of Kamehameha—buried there, Pu'uhonua o Hōnaunau, "Place of Refuge of Hōnaunau," survived the societal changes of 1819. Set aside as a national historical park in 1961, it is the only restored site of its kind. The 180-acre park is located twenty-two miles south of Kailua-Kona on the Big Island.

The park includes the six-acre pu'uhonua, which is located on a lava

► *A man blows a conch shell at the annual Establishment Day festival at Pu'uhonua o Hōnaunau National Historical Park on the Big Island.* GREG VAUGHN

► *The mortarless stone wall, left, beyond He-lei-pālala Fish Pond marks the boundaries of the sanctuary at Pu'uhonua o Hōnaunau.* MARNIE HAGMANN

► *A game board has been set up, right, for kō nane, an old Hawaiian "checkers" game, on the palace grounds at Pu'uhonua o Hōnaunau, an indication of the leisurely life enjoyed by the ali'i here.*
MARNIE HAGMANN

promontory and enclosed by an enormous, L-shaped stone wall, 1,000 feet long, ten feet high, and seventeen feet wide. Built about 1550 by master stonemasons, the wall was carefully fitted together without mortar. Kapu-breakers could swim across the bay into the sanctuary or enter overland. Individuals there for lengthy stays, such as those waiting out a war, foraged in the tidepools.

The centerpiece of the park is a heiau called Hale o Keawe, the mausoleum for the bones of the Keawe chiefs (*hale* means "house") and the source of mana for the sanctuary. By 1818 the bones of at least twenty-three Keawe chiefs had

been placed there, rendering it extremely powerful. The bones were removed to a secret resting place in 1829, but somehow an essence of their mana remains. In fact, visitors still leave offerings at the heiau.

Built around 1650 and reconstructed in 1968, Hale o Keawe is the most complete reproduction of its kind in the islands. Magnificently ferocious images, or *ki'i* carved from 'ōhi'a logs guard the heiau, which consists of a raised lava-rock platform topped by a thatched wooden framework. Other temples, both inside and outside the pu'uhonua enclosure, have not been rebuilt.

On the other side of the wall are the palace grounds. At least ten thatched

buildings once stood among the coconut palms here. The royal fish pond and a sandy beach reserved for the landing of royal canoes offer evidence of gracious, chiefly living. Farther south along the coast are the traces of two recreational slides, or *holua*. These slides were for royalty only—like sledding on grass and kukui-nut oil instead of ice.

Take plenty of time to visit Pu'uhonua o Hōnaunau. Enjoy a picnic in the shade of the old kiawe trees on the south side of the great wall and watch a furtive mongoose. There is an unmistakable, indefinable ambience here that contrasts pleasantly with that of the luxurious resorts just a few miles away.

Hawai'i Volcanoes National Park

► Dancers perform a hula for the royal court in a cultural reenactment during an Aloha Week celebration at Hawai'i Volcanoes National Park.

GREG VAUGHN

After the Marquesans, no one came to Hawai'i for hundreds of years. Then, in the thirteenth century, Polynesians from Tahiti, physically bigger and more robust than the earlier settlers, migrated to the islands.

One such visitor was Pā'ao. A man of great spiritual power, he was highly regarded by the natives and received as a chief. After spending some time in the islands, Pā'ao became critical of the ali'i, who, he believed, had weakened and degraded their bloodlines by mingling with commoners. He thought this compromised their divine right to rule.

Pā'ao returned to his homeland in the south to look for a chief potent enough to revivify the decadent ali'i and to strengthen their connections with the gods. He found a suitable candidate in Pili and brought him back to Hawai'i. Pili became the new chief, with Pā'ao as his high priest. Together they established a dynasty that ruled Hawai'i until the time of Kamehameha the Great and his high priest, Hewahewa.

Shortly after their arrival, Pā'ao

determined the most auspicious site for the construction of an important new temple, Waha'ula Heiau. Completed about 1275 and dedicated to the god of chiefs and war, this ''Temple of the Red Mouth''—the first of its kind in Hawai'i—required human sacrifices for its spiritual upkeep. The practice of building and maintaining *luakini,* or human sacrificial temples, spread from here throughout the islands and continued until the early nineteenth century.

Just inside the southern coastal entrance to Hawai'i Volcanoes National Park (or 27.5 miles from the Kīlauea Visitor Center via the Chain of Craters Road) stand the ruins of Waha'ula Heiau. At one time this heiau would have boasted an oracle tower covered in white kapa cloth; carved wooden statues; small thatched buildings for storing images, drums, and other equipment; and pits for disposing of broken or worn-out ceremonial gear. Now only the foundation remains.

► *These are some of the thousands of petroglyphs at Pu'uloa in Hawai'i Volcanoes National Park. The holes pictured here were chipped into the pāhoehoe lava to contain the umbilical stumps of infants in a ritual that foretold children's longevity.* DAVID MUENCH

Kealakekua Bay State Historical Park

One deity who did not care for human sacrifice was Lono, god of, among other things, agriculture and fertility. Peace-loving Lono preferred to be worshipped with feasting and celebration. Hawaiians accommodated Lono with extravagant religious observances during the Makahiki season from October to February.

At this time, any warlike activities ceased and people gathered to celebrate with food, athletic contests, hula festivals, general revelry, and parades. Priests carried images of Lono, long sticks draped with white kapa cloth, in processions heralding the god's symbolic return from his yearly travels. Chiefs collected taxes mostly in the form of food and gifts.

Hikiau Heiau, an important shrine of Lono, was the focus for many religious functions. Located near Nāpo'opo'o, its ruins are preserved in Kealakekua Bay State Historical Park.

A startling, unexpected guest at the Makahiki festival of 1779 was Captain James Cook, the first European to set foot on the islands. Cook had touched Hawaiian shores at Kaua'i the previous January, giving rise to speculation that he might somehow be connected to Lono. The coincidence of Cook's arriving in January two years in a row, the second time at such a sacred place, and in tall-masted, white-sailed ships that resembled the images carried in the processions, was powerfully suggestive. Not wanting to risk offending Lono, the Hawaiians, including a young ali'i named Kamehameha, accorded Cook every consideration.

After enjoying (and being somewhat bewildered by) Hawaiian hospitality, Cook set sail for his return voyage to England. A storm sent him back to Kealakekua Bay for repairs, but by this time, Cook/Lono had lost his luster for the Hawaiians. They killed him in a brief skirmish across the bay from the heiau. The site, marked by a white obelisk, is visible from the park.

▶ *A glowering wooden carving at Halape along the coast of Hawai'i Volcanoes National Park recalls the terrifying tikis of old.*
TOM BEAN

Pu'ukoholā Heiau National Historic Park

► *Thousands of workers handed these stones down from nearby hills to form the foundation of Pu'ukoholā Heiau.* DAVID MUENCH

Ali'i frequently commissioned heiau to be built to propitiate the gods before beginning a new enterprise. The chief called in an architect who looked at the possible sites and developed a model out of dirt or sand for the chief's approval. Before the work could begin, priests conducted a series of long and expensive ceremonies to obtain the aid of the gods and to ensure that the temple would be a suitable place for them to reside. Heiau dedicated to the war god Kū were the most elaborate and, as luakini, required human sacrifices to keep their mana powerful.

War was not uncommon in Hawai'i. Before Europeans arrived, the Hawaiians fought their enemies with clubs, wooden spears up to eighteen feet in length, shorter javelins, truncheons, bludgeons, daggers (sometimes lined with sharks' teeth), slingshots, and whatever else was at hand—rocks, sticks, or sand to throw in an opponent's eyes. They took quickly, however, to western-style cannons and guns and added them to their arsenals. Between real engagements, friendly chiefs would stage mock combats to keep their warriors fit and ready.

Pu'ukoholā Heiau, completed in 1791, was the last major religious construction of the ancient Hawaiian culture.

A famous prophet had said that Kamehameha, who had acquired enormous power and prestige as a warrior in the years since meeting Captain Cook, would conquer all the islands if he built a large temple to the war god Kū-kā'ili-moku atop Pu'ukoholā at Kawaihae on the Big Island. Kū-kā'ili-moku, a feathered image with a snarling mouth full of sharp teeth, was a powerful god, and Kamehameha ordered the construction at once. (This image may often be seen at the Bishop Museum in Honolulu.)

The work began in 1790, employing the prophet as the royal architect and thousands of laborers, including Kamehameha himself at times. The only person exempt was Kamehameha's younger brother, Keli'imaika'i, who had to remain ceremonially clean in order to preside at the religious services. Once, Keli'imaika'i picked up a stone to help. Kamehameha scolded him and had the stone taken out in a canoe beyond the horizon and dumped into the ocean. Every precaution was exercised—the temple had to be ritually perfect or it would not please the war god.

Forming a human chain, workers handed lava rocks down the mountainside. Some of the stones came from as far away as the Pololu Valley, fourteen miles distant. Constructed by carefully setting the waterworn lava rocks and boulders together without using mortar, the massive temple platform measured 224 by 100 feet. It had three walls, on the landward side and on either end. The side facing the sea was open and had three long, narrow, terraced steps across it.

Kamehameha completed his luakini in the summer of 1791 and invited his cousin and last rival on the Big Island, Keoua Kū-'ahu'ula, to the dedication ceremony. Keoua, perhaps resigned to his fate, accepted the ominous invitation. He and his entourage—carefully chosen old friends and high chiefs—were killed on the beach below the heiau as they stepped out of their canoes. Keoua's body was carried up to the heiau and placed on the altar as the principal sacrifice. Evidentally, the temple and the sacrifice pleased Kū-kā-'ili-moku, for Kamehameha went on to fulfull the prophecy. The temple was in use until 1819.

Mailekini Heiau, a temple—but not a luakini—used by Kamehameha's ancestors, is located below Pu'ukoholā Heiau. During Kamehameha's time it was used as a fort to protect the nearby village of Kawaihae. A third temple, Hale o Kapuni Heiau, dedicated to the shark gods, is believed to be submerged just offshore. The stone leaning post traditionally supported high chiefs who stood here to watch the sharks circling their offerings before devouring them.

Authorized by Congress August 17, 1972, seventy-seven-acre Pu'ukoholā Heiau National Historic Site is one mile away from Kawaihae and about twelve miles west of Waimea-Kohala.

► *A hula dancer, silhouetted against the sunset, is a timeless image of old Hawai'i.*
WILLIAM WATERFALL

Mo'okini Heiau State Monument

► As the sun sets across the 'Alenuihāhā Channel, Kamehameha I Birthsite State Monument, at the northern tip of the Big Island, is caught in a reflective mood. DAVID MUENCH

Twenty miles north of Kawaihae near Hawī, Mo'okini Heiau State Monument sprawls across a windy clearing. The size of a football field, Mo'okini, one of the most intact heiau in the islands, measures 267 feet at its longest point, 135 feet at its widest, and has outer walls thirty feet high. Inside, lower walls define passages, altars, foundations for thatched buildings (including one for the *mu,* or body-catcher), and ceremonial stones for the gods to enter.

Mo'okini is one of the oldest luakini, built soon after Pā'ao, the high priest of Waha'ula, introduced human sacrifice into the religious ceremonies. According to the ancient chants, the temple was dedicated in A.D. 480, though archaeologists estimate it was closer to 1250, by Kuamo'o Mo'okini, a high-ranking priest-chief from Tahiti. For the past 800 years the Mo'okini family has taken care of the temple, the only known heiau in Hawai'i whose high priest traces his or her descent from an unbroken line. Nearby, boulders mark Kamehameha I Birthsite State Monument. The stones are said to be the birthstones used in the ritual of his birth.

In 1978 the owners donated the land to the state on the condition that the heiau itself not be excavated. Then Leimomi Mo'okini Lum, the current priest, lifted an ancient kapu prohibiting outsiders from entering the heiau. The 3.2-acre park remains shrouded in mystery, but you can explore the temple and let your imagination do the excavating.

Haleki'i-Pihana Heiau State Monument

From a breezy hilltop covered with kiawe scrub, koa haole, and cactus, the magnificent view encompasses the West Maui Mountains, Haleakalā, Waihe'e, Wailuku, Kahului, and Kahului Bay. The hilltop also possesses two ruined heiau.

Haleki'i, or House of Images, was destroyed in the reforms of 1819 and reconstructed in 1958. The temple was used from 1765 to 1794, during the reign of Kahekili, the great chief of Maui. Kahekili, who was named for a god of thunder and had one side of his body tatooed black from head to toe as a reminder, was the last ruling chief of the island. He defended his kingdom from the armies of Kamehameha until his death in Waikiki in 1794.

A short distance away stand the ruins of Pihana Kalani, a former luakini. Both heiau were laid out on terraced stone platforms and had altars, kapa-covered oracle towers, and houses for the priest and king. Constructed of water-worn lava boulders and paved with pebbles, the terraces rose to heights between twelve and thirty feet.

Perhaps Kahekili's war god was not as powerful as Kamehameha's, or his sacrifices were not as pleasing. Kamehameha took Maui early in 1795. An air of defeat haunts this windy ten-acre park near Wailuku. If the heiau themselves are not inspiring, the view certainly is.

► *The ruins of Haleki'i Heiau in Haleki'i-Pihana Heiau State Monument overlook the West Maui Mountains.* LARRY ULRICH

'Ahu'ena Heiau

► *The 'Ahu'ena Heiau on the grounds of the Hotel King Kamehameha in Kailua-Kona has been faithfully restored. Typically, all that remains of such Hawaiian temples is a lava-rock platform.* GREG VAUGHN

Kamehameha fulfilled the prophecy of his military and political success, taking all the islands except Kaua'i by force. In 1810 he negotiated a settlement with the king of Kaua'i, thereby unifying all the island chiefdoms into one kingdom. In 1812, Hawai'i's greatest chief returned to Kamakahonu, across the bay from Kailua on the Big Island. He restored the temple, 'Ahu'ena Heiau, built houses, and spent the last seven years of his life there.

His conquests over, Kamehameha retired his war god and rededicated the heiau, a fifteenth-century luakini, to Lono, the god of peace, agriculture, and prosperity. Destroyed after Kamehameha's death, 'Ahu'ena was rebuilt in 1975 based on old drawings. Located on the grounds of the Hotel King Kamehameha and financed by Amfac Hotels, the $250,000 reconstruction is accurate except that the stone platform is slightly shorter than the original. Other details include three thatched houses, an oracle tower, and carved wooden images.

Other heiau

Like cathedral-hopping in Europe, visiting heiau in Hawai'i could be the basis for an entire vacation. The abundant ruins bespeak a fascinating culture that was all but swept away in 1819.

On Kaua'i, Hā'ena State Park has an early, complex, and extensive archaeological site, including Lohiau's Dancing Platform, which is a heiau dedicated to Laka, goddess of the hula, and Ka ulu Paoa Heiau overlooking Ke'e Beach. Along the banks of the Wailua River, the Wailua Complex of Heiau (a National Historic Landmark) includes the rubble of ancient heiau, a pu'uhonua, birthstones, and a bellstone.

About a mile from Wai'ānapanapa State Park on Maui, the Wai'ānapanapa-Hana coastal trail, of archaeological interest itself as an ancient Hawaiian footpath, passes a ruined heiau and some building foundations.

On O'ahu, Keaī wa Heiau State Recreation Area at the end of 'Aiea Heights Drive in 'Aiea, not far from Honolulu, preserves the remains of a heiau ho'ola, a temple of healing, and has traditional Hawaiian medicinal plants on display. At an elevation of 1,000 feet, the 384.5-acre recreation area features a cool, pleasant climate, a 4.8-mile loop trail through a eucalyptus forest, and picnicking and camping facilities. Across the island, the gigantic Pu'u o Mahuka Heiau dominates a bluff overlooking Waimea Bay. O'ahu's largest heiau, once a luakini and now a National Historic Landmark, includes a platform with two adjoining smaller structures. In Kailua, overlooking Kawainui Marsh, the ruins of Ulu Po Heiau are preserved as a state monument. Archaeologists have recently determined that the marsh was occupied between A.D. 700 and 900.

Kāneakē Heiau in the Mākaha Valley is not always open to visitors due to uncertain road conditions. Restored to its pre-1819 appearance by the Bishop Museum, complete with thatched buildings, the temple rivals Hale o Keawe at Pu'uhonua o Hōnaunau for visual excitement. Contact the Sheraton Mākaha Resort for information.

► *Stones wrapped in ti leaves adorn the altar at Pu'u Mahuka Heiau State Monument, right, O'ahu's largest ancient temple. Previous offerings here may have included a watering party commanded by Captain George Vancouver in 1793.* ED COOPER

► *Wailua River State Park on Kaua'i, once a seat of chiefly power, is rich in archaeological relics such as these birthstones, right, where the umbilical cords of newborn ali'i were hidden.*
MARNIE HAGMANN

Kahana Valley State Park

Life in Hawai'i naturally involved much more than the religious ceremonies of the priests and the military adventures of the chiefs. The majority of the people, the commoners, lived relatively simple lives as farmers or fishermen.

The islands were divided into districts, or *moku,* whose boundaries still exist in today's administrative divisions. Several districts, or even an entire island (and eventually, under Kamehameha, all the islands), were ruled by one ali'i, the high chief. The districts were further divided into wedges of land, *ahupua'a,* and ruled by lesser chiefs. Ahupua'a were pie-shaped, extending from the beach to the mountains, to provide a balanced economy of forest, agricultural, and ocean products.

Commoners could not own property in the ahupua'a, but they were given the privilege of working the land. People in the uplands raised sweet potatoes, yams, sugarcane, bananas, breadfruit, ti, and taro. Those along the coast raised coconut palms and fish. Taxes, in the form of food, animals, and items such as adzes, woven mats, bowls, and kapa, were collected each year during the Makahiki festival. The local chief collected two portions from each family, one to support himself and the other to send on to the king. With these taxes, the chiefs constructed temples and irrigation projects,

supported the priests who staffed the temples, and paid for expensive ceremonial objects.

Kahana Valley State Park, twenty-six miles from Honolulu along the Kamehameha Highway on windward O'ahu, is one of the few publicly owned ahupua'a remaining in Hawai'i. Its 140 residents live in a traditional way, demonstrating the Hawaiian concepts of *kokua* (mutual help or assistance) and *ohana* (family values). Visitors should respect the privacy of the people living in the valley, not trespass on their property, and follow the park rules.

Covering 5,220 acres, the ahupua'a extends from sea level at Huilua Fish Pond to 2,670 feet at Pu'u Pauao on the crest of the Ko'olau Range.

Huilua, the park's most impressive archaeological site and a National Historic Landmark, is a fish pond at the end of Kahana Stream. Following the natural curvature of the shoreline, the graceful seawalls once enclosed mullet ('ama'ama) and milkfish (awa) in the calm, brackish waters.

Shallow Kahana Bay affords perfect conditions for fishing by the traditional *hukilau* method. Fishing this way calls for a group of fishermen and a long net, typically with floats along the upper edge and weights along the bottom. With some fishermen holding one end of the net in place on the shore, the others pull

the opposite end out and around the fish to another point farther down the beach. The men pull the net slowly to shore with large ropes dangling ti leaves (the leaves help prevent the fish from swimming out of the trap). As the shrinking semicircle draws tighter, all kinds of fish are caught. Anyone who wets his feet during the netting gets a share of the catch.

Archaeologists believe a wet taro system once dominated the Kahana Valley. Now 120 small wet terraces and twelve irrigation canals survive. The current residents raise taro, bananas, and vegetables.

Two hiking trails, always muddy (Pu'u Pauao, at the head of the valley, receives an average of 300 inches of rain a year), lead deep into the mountains. Wild pigs, which can be hunted here on weekends and holidays, roam through a thick forest of 'ōhi'a, hala, breadfruit, bamboo, mountain apple, guava, and other trees. For the ancient Hawaiians, the mountains were the source of water, useful plants, and wood.

Visiting Kahana Valley today, with its perpetually overcast skies, banana groves, taro patches, glistening forests, and steep mountains, one appreciates the proximity of the natural and supernatural worlds of the Hawaiians. Perhaps capricious spirits and ghosts still inhabit these woods and fields.

Lapakahi State Historical Park

For 500 years Hawaiians lived in black stone huts with golden thatched roofs at Lapakahi, the oceanfront section of an ahupua'a near the northern tip of the Big Island. Now the houses are empty and in ruins, but 262-acre Lapakahi State Historical Park comes to life with cultural demonstrations, storytelling, and a self-guided walk through the village.

Scattered artifacts—fishing gear, a game board, small shrines, a fire pit, the rocks used to evaporate salt from seawater (this salt was an important source of iron in the ancient Hawaiians' diet)—and plantings of endemic and Polynesian species—beach naupaka, hala, milo, kou, paper mulberry, breadfruit—contribute to the authenticity of this partial restoration.

Apparently, Lapakahi was not attractive to ali'i. Existence here was hard. The thin, dry soil was fertile but required backbreaking effort to cultivate. Above the village, farmers terraced the hillside to raise sweet potatoes, gourds, and sugarcane. Windbreaks kept the crops from blowing away in the strong Kohala winds. As the village became more prosperous, some families moved into the Kohala Mountains, and the ahupua'a was established.

The real wealth of the ahupua'a came from the sea. Along the rocky shore, villagers caught mollusks, crustaceans, and fish in fish traps. They gathered *limu*, or seaweed, for food, medicine,

▶ The life of Lapakahi, an ancient fishing village, is strongly suggested by various scattered artifacts and these stones, which mark its house sites. ED COOPER

► *Poi pounders, like these displayed at Lapakahi State Historical Park on the Big Island, were used to pound taro roots into poi, the starchy staple of the Hawaiian diet.* GREG VAUGHN

ornamentation, fish bait, and sometimes for religious rituals.

From the shore, a fisherman might throw a cast net, a circular one-man net weighted at the rim, over a school of tasty *manini,* a type of surgeonfish. The net, designed to fall face down on the water, traps the fish as it sinks to the bottom.

The pebbly coral beach at Lapahaki is one of the few places along the rugged leeward coast from which canoes could be safely launched and landed. Nowadays, fishing boats ply the entire lee side of the island for game species and food fish such as *ono* (meaning "to have sweet taste") and *'ahi,* the delicious yellowfin tuna, but the waters off Lapakahi comprise a marine life conservation district (MLCD). Fishing (except for *'ōpelu,* or mackerel scad) and removing or disturbing any marine life or geological feature are prohibited.

A visit to Lapakahi connects you with the past. Pause at the stone that was a home of Ku'ula, the fishing god, where fishermen always left a portion of their catch. Observe the fishing spears, fish traps, hooks, octopus lures, bait pounders, and nets strewn about the village. Sit at the game board atop the bluff where generations of fishermen passed the time watching the sea and waiting for the afternoon winds to die down. The Hawaiians could read the flights of birds, the shifting colors of the water, the patterns of waves and currents. For them the information might have launched a fishing party; for us, scanning the horizon seems like an old human habit.

Other cultural parks

Remnants of ancient Hawaiian culture are scattered throughout the islands. Many are subtle or unintelligible to the untrained eye. Petroglyphs, those evocative writings on rock, may not be completely understandable, but they still communicate something to the viewer. Only a few parks preserve examples of petroglyphs, such as Hawai'i Volcanoes National Park.

Fish ponds are a more accessible vestige of traditional Hawaiian life. Built to husband shore-dwelling fish, such as mullet and awa, the walls of fish ponds were made of coral blocks and lava rocks and sometimes rose six feet above the water. Narrow wooden gratings allowed small fish to enter. Once fattened and full grown, they were too large to escape, providing a convenient meal for villagers. Some fish ponds still function; many more have been silted in, destroyed by tidal waves, or removed by developers.

Good examples exist on O'ahu, which once had ninety-seven fish ponds but now has only a few. On the windward side of the island, in addition to Huilua Fish Pond at Kahana Valley State Park, are the Kahalu'u Fish Pond at Kahalu'u Beach Park; He'eia Fish Pond, O'ahu's biggest, with a retaining wall twelve feet wide and 5,000 feet long, enclosing eighty-eight acres of water (and mangrove swamp) at He'eia State Park; and Moli'i Fish Pond, with a 4,000-foot retaining wall, at the south end of Kualoa Beach Park.

(Privately owned Moli'i is still in use.) On the south shore, Pearl Harbor was once the site of many fish ponds. Some are now on government property, but from Blaisdell Memorial Park, you can view a fish pond that was once a huge, protected area for crabbing and fishing.

Near Lihu'e on Kaua'i, the Alakoko Fish Pond is an example of an unusual freshwater pond, which was formed by cutting off an elbow of the Hule'ia Stream. No longer in use, the pond is said to have been built by the menehunes, Hawai'i's legendary "little people."

Moloka'i has a large concentration of fish ponds on the south shore along the Kamehameha V Highway, many dating from the fifteenth century. Nearly sixty of these royal fish ponds once provided a steady supply of mullet for ali'i. Two are national historical landmarks—Ke'awa-nui, which covers almost fifty-five acres, and 'Ualapu'e, twenty-two acres.

On the Kona coast of the Big Island, Kaloko Honokōhau National Historical Park preserves three historical fish ponds—'Ai'makapa, Ka-loko, and 'Ai'opio—and will restore one of them, Ka-loko, to its original appearance and function. In addition to the ponds, the area contains 234 known historical and archaeological sites, possibly including (according to one tradition) the burial site of Kamehameha the Great.

The old ways changed irrevocably when Captain Cook put in at Kealakekua

Bay. But faint echoes of ancient Hawaiian life linger in places such as Lapakahi and Kahana Valley, in the grim ruins of heiau, in the ineffable spiritual power of Pu'uhonua o Hōnaunau. The old Hawaiian presence is everywhere, if one is only sensitive to it. ■

► *A weaver at Pu'uhonua o Hōnaunau National Historic Park plaits sandals of ti leaves, keeping an ancient art alive.*
GREG VAUGHN

Chapter four

Historical Hawai'i

"Ambition leads me not only farther than any other man has been before me, but as far as I think it is possible for a man to go."

—Captain James Cook

Captain James Cook (1728-1779), son of a Scottish farm laborer, knew how far man could go in the eighteenth century because he had been there. A man of little education beyond reading, writing, and arithmetic, he had a natural aptitude for mathematics and astronomy and a deep curiosity about the natural world. The British Royal Society sent him to the Pacific on three voyages: the first to Tahiti to observe the transit of Venus across the sun to provide data for better celestial navigation; the second—one of the greatest discovery voyages in history, covering more than seventy thousand miles—to circumnavigate the globe at the southernmost latitude possible to see if there was a habitable continent there; and the third to look for the mythical Northwest Passage between the Atlantic and Pacific oceans.

For this last assignment, Cook set sail from England in 1777 with two ships, the *Resolution* and the *Discovery*. He sailed south along the coast of Africa, rounded the Cape of Good Hope, crossed the Indian Ocean, continued east through Cook Strait between the islands of New Zealand, and headed northeast. On January 18, 1778, he sighted O'ahu, and on the twentieth, he anchored off Waimea, Kaua'i, near today's Waimea State Recreation Pier. The ships traded for fresh water and food, and, despite Cook's best efforts to prevent it, the favors of Hawaiian women.

On February 2 the Europeans departed for Alaska, leaving behind seeds, goats, and venereal diseases that would contribute to irreversible changes in the islands and their people. After seven months of exploring the southern coast of Alaska, the Bering Sea, and venturing into the Arctic Ocean, where he was stopped by ice, Cook satisfied himself that no navigable passage to the Atlantic existed and returned to Hawai'i.

He anchored off the Big Island in Kealakekua Bay. If the Hawaiians were friendly his first time through, this time, exactly a year later, they greeted him with boundless enthusiasm. They identified him with the god Lono. At Hikiau Heiau, the great temple of Lono in what is now Kealakekua Bay State Historical Park, the priests offered reverence to Cook as though he were a god. For two weeks during the annual Makahiki festival, he and his men enjoyed the extravagant hospitality of the natives.

On February 4 the *Discovery* and the *Resolution* sailed along the Kona coast to the north. At Kawaihae Bay, where Kamehameha would build his great war temple, Pu'ukoholā Heiau, eleven years later, Cook looked for but could not find a suitable anchorage. The weather turned bad, one of the *Resolution*'s masts broke in gale-force winds, and both ships returned to Kealakekua Bay for repairs on February 10. There Cook found that the emotional climate had cooled—for reasons that are still not well understood, he was no longer a god-king in the Hawaiians' eyes.

When the Hawaiians stole one of the ships' boats, an exasperated Cook went ashore with a contingent of marines. His plan was to take a hostage against the return of the boat, a maneuver that had worked to good effect in similar situations elsewhere in the Pacific. This time, however, it failed because the hostage, an old chief, would not willingly accompany him back to the *Resolution*. The crowd on the beach attacked the Englishmen, and someone stabbed Cook in the back of the neck. The surging warriors clubbed and stabbed him repeatedly and held him face-down in the water. Some of the marines made it back to the ship, but they had to leave Cook's body behind.

A few days later, after a reading of the naval burial service and a cannon salute, Cook's bones—those that had been returned—were consigned to the waters of Kealakekua Bay. A hundred years later, a marker—a white obelisk visible from the state park—was erected on the shore at the spot where he had fallen, a belated tribute to a man who had braved Arctic and Antarctic ice, coral reefs, tropical storms, and intransigent natives, and had managed and protected the health of crews on voyages lasting years.

On February 22 the *Discovery* and the *Resolution* hoisted anchor. No one called again in Hawaiian waters until 1785.

After that first contact with Europeans, Hawai'i was brought into the modern era. The past two hundred years have been eventful, turbulent, and sometimes tragic. Hawai'i preserves this history in monuments such as the U.S.S. *Arizona* Memorial, commemorating the infamy of Pearl Harbor; the State Capitol, a

► *Wreathed in eighteen-foot lei of flowers and maile for Kamehameha Day (June 11), a bronze statue of the great chief stands across from 'Iolani Palace.* GREG VAUGHN/ TOM STACK & ASSOCIATES.

► *This obelisk at Kealakekua Bay on the Big Island commemorates Captain James Cook, who died here in 1779.* GREG VAUGHN

culmination of the long road to statehood; and 'Iolani Palace, evoking the glitter and sad decline of the Hawaiian monarchy. Some elements of the story persist in Hawai'i's parklands in unexpected ways—in a sculpture or garden or forest. A few pages of the historical record (those concerning whaling, for example) are missing from the parks entirely, but they can be found elsewhere, safeguarded and interpreted by organizations such as the Lahaina Restoration Foundation. Even with gaps, Hawai'i's parklands tell a fascinating story of the past.

Pu'ukoholā Heiau National Historic Site

One of the chiefs on hand to greet Captain Cook at Kealakekua Bay was the young ali'i Kamehameha. A warrior and strategist, he would later unify the islands and found the kingdom of Hawai'i.

By 1790 Kamehameha ruled the northwestern half of the Big Island and had invaded and conquered Maui, Lāna'i, and Moloka'i. O'ahu and Kaua'i held out, and on the Big Island, one rival chief, his cousin Keoua Kū'ahu'ula, remained.

Kamehameha would have all the islands, a prophet said, if he constructed a temple to his family war god. The temple, Pu'ukoholā Heiau, was started. Volcano goddess Pele indicated her approval—or so it seemed to the Hawaiians—when a freak explosion of Kīlauea, in what is now Hawai'i Volcanoes National Park, killed a band of Keoua's warriors and their entourage.

Despite the omen, the not-completely-subdued chiefs of Maui, Lāna'i, and Moloka'i joined the chiefs of Kaua'i and O'ahu, and they all sailed to attack Kamehameha. Although distracted by the exacting demands of temple construction, the great warrior fended off his adversaries and completed the structure.

In the summer of 1791, the sacrifice of Cousin Keoua at the dedication ceremony launched Kamehameha's campaign. About 1794 he reconquered Maui, Lāna'i, and Moloka'i. O'ahu fell in the spring of 1795 in the Battle of Nu'uanu, which is commemorated at Nu'uanu Pali State Wayside. With this victory, Kamehameha established his kingdom. Kaua'i held out until 1810 for a negotiated peace.

In addition to the war temple and two other heiau, Pu'ukoholā Heiau National Monument protects the John Young house site, a ruined dwelling hidden in the kiawe scrub on the hill behind the heiau. Young, a British sailor stranded on Hawai'i in 1790, became a trusted advisor to Kamehameha. Called Olohana (''all hands'') in Hawaiian and made a chief, he married a niece of Kamehameha, served as governor of the Big Island from 1802 to 1812, and acted as business agent for the king. His granddaughter Emma

► *The sun sets at Kawaihae near the site of Kamehameha's Pu'ukoholā Heiau.* JOHN J. SMITH

married King Kamehameha IV.

Nearby in Kawaihae is the site of Pelekāne, Kamehameha's residence for a time. His son Liholiho returned here after his father's death in 1819 to prepare for his role as King Kamehameha II, ruler of all the Hawaiian islands. Six months later, Liholiho and Ka'ahumanu, Kamehameha the Great's favorite of his twenty-one wives, abolished the Hawaiian religion and kapu system. At 'Ahu'ena Heiau in Kailua-Kona, Liholiho ordered the desecration of the temples. Only those heiau serving as temple-mausoleums, such as Hale o Keawe at Pu'uhonua o Hōnaunau, were spared.

Hawai'i Volcanoes National Park

In 1819, not long after public worship of Hawaiian gods was officially banned, Christian missionaries sailed from New England to bring their God to the islands. But having just shed their old religion, the Hawaiians were slow to accept him. Gradually the missionaries won converts. A major victory came in 1824 when the ali'i Kapi'olani decided to affirm her new belief in Christianity and show her people that Pele no longer had any power.

Ignoring the warnings of kahuna, Kapi'olani descended into the caldera of Kilauea. Standing at the brink of Halema'uma'u, at that time a lake of molten lava, she chewed 'ōhelo berries (sacred to Pele) and spit them into the pit. Everyone expected Pele to react violently to the insult, but nothing happened. Kapi'olani's courage and Pele's inertness struck a deathblow to the old order.

Some resistance to the Christianizing influence of the missionaries came from the men aboard sailing ships, which called regularly in Hawaiian waters after 1785. After months at sea, missionary morality was far less interesting to sailors than uninhibited Hawaiian women.

► *Steam vents have replaced the lake of fire that the ali'i Kapi'olani faced in defiance of Pele at Halema'uma'u Crater in Hawai'i Volcanoes National Park.* TOM BEAN

In addition to women, an important item of commerce in Hawai'i was sandalwood, which was in great demand in Canton for incense and furniture manufacture. Captain John Kendrick, a pioneering American trader, noticed sandalwood growing on Kaua'i in 1791 and contracted for several cargoes. Kamehameha I, aware of Hawai'i's extensive groves of sandalwood, forced commoners by the thousands into the mountains to retrieve it. Vast quantities of the fragrant wood were shipped to China between 1810 and 1825 as Hawai'i's first major export.

Sandalwood gave the infant kingdom its start in the commercial world, and Kamehameha's extravagance almost ended it. For example, when sandalwood was traded for a ship, the correct amount was determined by digging a pit of the same dimensions as the vessel and filling it with sandalwood logs. (Such a pit remains in the Moloka'i Forest Reserve.) The slow-growing trees, despite their abundance, could not withstand the pressure. By 1840 sandalwood, at least in commercial quantities, was gone. Now there are only remnants of the old groves.

"An aura of romance, ignorance, and mystery surrounds the sandalwood tree in Hawai'i," wrote Territorial Forester C.S. Judd in 1932. The Hawaiians, who called it *'ili-ahi*, applied sandalwood bark as a remedy for lice and used powdered heartwood to perfume kapa. There is a stand of the trees on the Sandalwood Trail (1.5 miles), which starts near Volcano House.

Russian Fort Elizabeth State Park

One offshoot of the sandalwood trade was the short-lived Russian presence in Hawai'i. Russian ships came to Hawai'i as early as 1804, and the possibility of a Russian settlement, like Fort Ross in California, was discussed from time to time. In 1815 the Russian-American Company sent Georg Anton Schaeffer, a German-born surgeon, to Hawai'i to recover the cargo of a Russian ship wrecked on Kaua'i or at least get compensation for it.

Schaeffer, a man with his own sense of mission, presented himself at the court of Kamehameha, posing as a botanist. Once he gained the king's confidence, he not only brought up the question of salvage but also discussed trading privileges. Kamehameha granted the Russian-American Company a monopoly on sandalwood and other concessions, and Schaeffer went off to meet with Kaumuali'i, the king of Kaua'i.

Although Kaumuali'i had agreed in 1810 to acknowledge Kamehameha's sovereignty, he still nursed grievances. Schaeffer, ever flexible, changed his strategy to take advantage of Kaumuali'i's disaffection with Kamehameha. Schaeffer promised Kaumuali'i arms to recover Kaua'i and take over Maui, O'ahu, Lāna'i, and Moloka'i, in return for land and sandalwood.

In preparation for his new career as an island baron, Schaeffer started the construction of a fort at the mouth of

Kaua'i's Waimea River. His scheme, however, lacked the support of the Russian--American Company and of mother Russia, and he was hounded out of Hawai'i by American traders in July 1817.

After Schaeffer's embarrassed departure, the Hawaiian army took over and completed the Russian Fort Elizabeth and occupied it until 1864. Now in ruins, the fort is a convenient stop on the way to Waimea Canyon and Kōke'e state parks. The seventeen-acre site features a self-guided walk through the rubble under the shade of graceful old kiawe trees.

► Visitors take a self-guided tour through the crumbled remains at Russian Fort Elizabeth State Historical Park on Kaua'i. The fort was abandoned by the Russians in 1817, and used by the Hawaiian government until 1864. MICHAEL S. SAMPLE

Kalaupapa National Historical Park

► *Surf thunders along the coastline of Kalaupapa National Historical Park in northern Moloka'i.* RICHARD A. COOKE III

As the sandalwood trade waned, whaling replaced it as the basis of the Hawaiian economy. Then sugar cultivation succeeded whaling. After the first western-style sugar plantation was established on Kaua'i in 1835, the sugar business grew quickly. In 1875 King Kalākaua, the Hawaiian monarch at the time, signed a treaty of commercial reciprocity with the United States. The treaty permitted Hawaiian sugar to enter the states duty-free, giving island producers a competitive advantage in the American market. In return, the United States was given the use of Pearl Harbor.

During the boom years, planters had trouble finding enough men to work in the cane fields. The native Hawaiian population had declined from approximately 300,000 at the time of Cook to fewer than 60,000 by the early 1880s. Introduced diseases, against which the Hawaiians had no immunity, had taken a heavy toll.

One of the diseases was leprosy. First observed in the islands in 1830, it was called *mai pake,* or "come from China disease," in Hawaiian. By 1865 it was so prevalent that an "Act to Prevent the Spread of Leprosy" was signed into law by King Kamehameha V. Under the new law, people with the disease were relocated to the isolated Kalaupapa peninsula on the northern coast of Moloka'i. On January 6, 1866, the first group was transported there aboard the government schooner *Warwick*.

In 1868 Norwegian scientist Armauer Hansen identified the bacteria causing leprosy, which has come to be known as Hansen's disease. But very little was known about the way it was transmitted from person to person. Many whites thought the disease was a judgment against the Hawaiian people. The government did everything it could to find a cure for leprosy, but nothing worked. By the end of the 1870s more than a thousand people had been sent to Moloka'i.

In 1873 a young Belgian priest, Father Damien Joseph de Veuster, came to the island. He lived among the afflicted fearlessly, and, some said, without common sense. He was officially diagnosed in 1885 as having the disease, and he died four years later at the age of forty-nine. His contributions to improving the conditions—physical, mental, and spiritual—for those living at Kalaupapa have earned him a lasting place in the history of Hawai'i and in the history of one of the world's oldest and most terrifying diseases. A statue of Father Damien stands near the State Capitol, a reminder of his life and work on Moloka'i.

By the 1940s, sulfone drugs had been developed to treat Hansen's disease, and patients no longer need to be isolated from the rest of the population. Today about a hundred people, most between the ages of fifty and eighty, reside voluntarily at Kalaupapa.

Created by Congress in 1980, Kalaupapa National Historical Park is a monument to the courage of victims of Hansen's disease. It sounds unlikely, but visiting Kalaupapa and talking to its residents is spiritually satisfying and uplifting. To visit the park you must take a guided tour, be at least sixteen years old, and have a permit from the Hawai'i State Department of Health or the National Park Service. Access is limited by geography to travel on foot, by mule, or by airplane.

► *The original burial site of Father Damien Joseph de Veuster, who martyred himself tending to victims of Hansen's disease, adjoins St. Philomena's Catholic Church in Kalawao.* RICHARD A. COOKE III

► *The Moloka'i coast, above, dwarfs Father Damien's church on the Kalaupapa Peninsula.*
MARGARETTE MEAD

► *The Royal Mausoleum State Monument, right, in Nu'uanu Valley houses the remains of nineteenth century Hawaiian royalty.* MARNIE HAGMANN

Pālā'au State Park

Overlooking the peninsula from 2,000-foot, fortress-like cliffs, Pālā'au State Park offers a magnificent view of Kalaupapa National Historical Park and an alternative to the arduous trip down.

Wave erosion carved the steep, former sea cliffs, but a volcano in Moloka'i's recent geological past halted the process and created the peninsula, a flat tongue of land. Its relative inaccessibility made it suitable for resettling victims of Hansen's disease.

In addition to the excellent view and the National Park Service interpretive signs, the 234-acre state park features a phallic stone, believed by ancient Hawaiians to enhance fertility.

Royal Mausoleum State Monument

When Kamehameha the Great died in 1819, two trusted companions hid his bones in a secret place to prevent them from being defiled by power seekers. "The morning star alone knows where Kamehameha's bones are guarded," they said. Later monarchs did not require secret burials, and in 1825 the first royal mausoleum was constructed to house the remains of King Kamehameha II and Queen Kamamalu, who died of measles (normally not fatal, but the Hawaiians had no resistance) while visiting England.

The original mausoleum, located on the grounds of the future 'Iolani Palace in Honolulu, filled up over the years with royal remains. By 1865 it was too crowded, and the ali'i were moved to a new and larger mausoleum in Nu'uanu Valley.

This ten-acre burial ground, with its chapel newly restored, is the final resting place of the Kings Kamehameha II to V, King Kalākaua, and his successor and sister Lili'uokalani, and Charles Reed Bishop and his wife, Bernice Pauahi Paki, who was a great granddaughter of Kamehameha I. (Her land trust, The Bishop Estate, today supports the Kamehameha Schools for children of Hawaiian blood.)

Only William Charles Lunalilo, who reigned fourteen months in 1872-74, lies in a private tomb on the grounds of the historical Kawaiaha'o Church in downtown Honolulu. He considered himself "the people's king" and wanted to be buried with "the people he loved."

'Iolani Palace State Monument

When King Kalākaua came to power in 1874, he decided that the modest house the Hawaiian monarchs had lived in since the mid-1840s was unsuitable. He needed a luxurious palace that would match his personal eminence.

Construction began on the new royal residence in 1879. Four years later it was completed and furnished for the then-kingly sum of $360,000. The combined efforts of three architects resulted in 'Iolani Palace, a grey-and-white building described as "American Florentine," with blonde wood trim, wide balconies, and spacious rooms. Finished with red velvet draperies, gilt-framed mirrors, Douglas-fir floors, a seven-foot marble bath, a curving staircase, and many other amenities, it was lavish enough for the king.

The palace, which measures 140 feet by 100 feet, has two main floors; a basement with kitchens, storerooms, and offices for the household staff; and a large attic. A wide hall dominates the first floor, running the entire width of the building. On the right as you enter is the Throne Room, and on the left are the Blue Room and the Dining Room. Upstairs are the royal family's living quarters, with King Kalākaua's suite on the left and Queen Kapi'olani's on the right. The queen found palace life not entirely to her taste and kept a private residence as well.

The new palace may have given the king, who staged an elaborate coronation

▶ *On the grounds of 'Iolani Palace, wrought iron and ti plants enclose the site of the first royal mausoleum and crypt, built in 1825. The palace itself was completed in 1883.* ED COOPER

► *A statue of Queen Lili'uokalani, Hawai'i's last reigning monarch, stands regally upon the grounds of the State Capitol.* DOUGLAS PEEBLES

day for himself on February 12, 1883, a sense of having more power than the sugarcane planters and businessmen wanted him to have. A revolution and a new constitution, signed in the Blue Room on July 6, 1887, reduced Kalākaua to a figurehead, allowed to reign but not rule.

In July 1889 a short-lived counter-revolution, led by royalist Robert W. Wilcox, briefly gave Kalākaua hope that the old order could be restored. It wasn't, and Wilcox died in California in January 1891 of complications resulting from a stroke. His body was brought back to Hawai'i and buried in the Royal Mausoleum.

Since Kalākaua died childless, and since his brother had died in 1877, the next in line for the throne was his sister, fifty-two-year-old Lili'uokalani. A complicated woman with a talent for music (she wrote "Aloha Oe"), Lili'uokalani swore to uphold the constitution of 1887, but she had her own ideas about how to rule her kingdom. In 1893 fears that she would take the constitution into her own hands led to her arrest, the end of the Hawaiian monarchy, and the formation of the Republic of Hawai'i.

The queen was found guilty of high treason when national guardsmen found an ammunition dump in the flower garden of Washington Place, her home before she ascended to the throne and now the official residence of the governor. She was fined $5,000 and sentenced to five years of hard labor. Her sentence was reduced, however, to house arrest and a period of confinement to her apartments at the palace.

From 1893 to 1968, 'Iolani Palace was used as the capitol for the republic, the territory, and finally the state of Hawai'i. (The Senate convened in the Dining Room and the House of Representatives in the Throne Room.) When the new state capitol was completed in 1969, the Friends of 'Iolani Palace, with state funding, began the job of restoring the much-abused, termite-ridden building to its former grandeur. The job took $6 million and six years.

Today visitors, shod in floor-protecting slippers provided at the door, can admire the interior of the palace under the watchful guidance of docents. Outside, the coronation pavilion, the old mausoleum with its plantings of ti and ginger, and the beautifully landscaped grounds invite quiet exploration in the middle of Honolulu.

Kapa'a Beach Park

Hawai'i solved the problem of labor shortages in the cane fields by importing workers from China, Japan, Korea, the Philippines, and Portugal. The ethnic diversity that resulted was one reason the United States hesitated to confer statehood on the territory. Each immigrant group has had a fascinating history in the islands, and each has contributed to the richness of Hawai'i today.

The bombing of Pearl Harbor made life very difficult for Hawaiian Japanese, because few people believed the attack could have succeeded without the help of local Japanese. In order not to be deemed disloyal to the United States, the Japanese had to be extremely circumspect. For example, on Kaua'i a statue commemorating the Russo-Japanese War of 1904-5 was buried to prevent its being misunderstood during World War II. The monument was exhumed a few years ago and for the time being, stands in the soccer field at Kapa'a Beach Park.

U.S.S. *Arizona* Memorial

Japan did, of course, have spies in Hawai'i. One of the best was Takeo Yoshikawa, an unobtrusive, twenty-eight-year-old ensign in the Japanese naval reserve. Assigned to the Japanese consulate in Honolulu in March 1941, Yoshikawa played the role of conscientious tourist impeccably. From 'Aiea Heights in the hills behind Pearl Harbor, which he visited thirty times in two months, he observed the comings and goings of ships, the routines of the harbor, and the habits of sailors. In particular, he noticed their behavior on weekends, paying close attention to their boisterous Saturday nights and quiet, slow-to-get-started Sunday mornings. His information was extremely useful to the Japanese navy.

Early Sunday morning, December 7, 1941, while most people were sleeping, the Japanese struck Pearl Harbor, Hickam Airfield, Kaneohe Naval Air Station, Bellows Airfield, Ewa Marine Corps Air Station, Schofield Barracks, and Wheeler Airfield. The unprecedented attack—the greatest military defeat in American history—crippled the Pacific Fleet, killed 2,403 people and wounded 1,178

(Japanese losses were approximately 129), and catapulted the United States into World War II.

Eight U.S. ships were sunk or beached, and thirteen were badly damaged. With the exception of the U.S.S. *Arizona,* the U.S.S. *Utah,* and the U.S.S. *Oklahoma,* all were salvaged and later saw action. At the airfields, 188 aircraft were destroyed and 159 damaged. The Japanese lost six ships, including five midget submarines and one I-Class submarine, and twenty-nine aircraft. Another seventy-four aircraft were damaged.

The U.S.S. *Arizona* sustained the most damage. At 8:10 a.m. the battleship was hit by a 1,760-pound armor-piercing bomb that exploded near the forward magazines, detonating more than one million pounds of ammunition. The tremendous fireball instantly killed 1,177 sailors and marines and sank the ship within nine minutes. Only about 330 survived.

The *Arizona* was so badly damaged in the assault that it would never sail again. While other ships were repaired, the *Arizona* lay in the harbor, a silent admonition to a nation unprepared for

war. Built in the New York Navy Yard in Brooklyn, New York, launched in 1915, and commissioned in 1916, the ship was decommissioned in 1942 and taken off the official registry of warships.

Two years after the raid, the navy had the opportunity to raise the ship and possibly recover the dead, but at an enormous cost. Medical examiners advised against it, saying the men would be unrecognizable. The tomb was left undisturbed.

Since 1950 the *Arizona* has been in "symbolic commission" and has flown the U.S. flag. The Pacific Fleet render honors whenever they pass the wreck. The memorial, which stands over the wreck, was dedicated on Memorial Day 1962. Today nearly a million and a half visitors annually come to pay personal tribute to the men who lost their lives here.

Visitors ride a shuttle boat out to the memorial, which looks like a sagging covered bridge and is composed of three sections: the bell room, which is the primary location for viewing the deck of the sunken *Arizona*; the assembly room, which can accommodate 200 people for ceremonies; and the shrine room, where

► *The American flag still flies above the ghostly remains of the U.S.S.* Arizona *in Pearl Harbor, honoring the battleship's symbolic commission.*
DOUGLAS PEEBLES

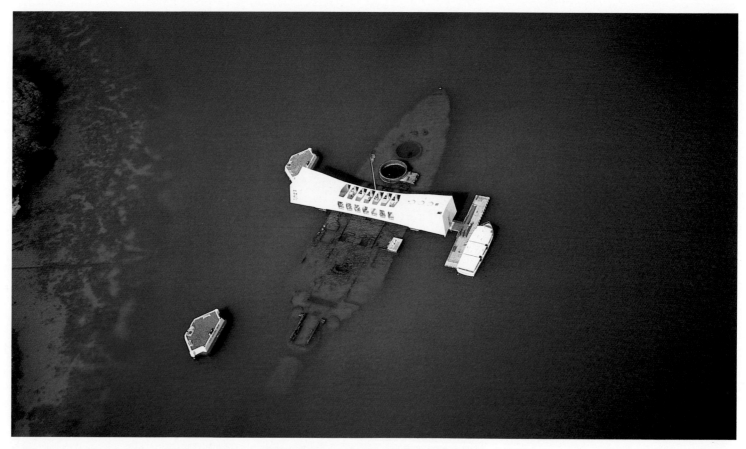

the names of the 1,177 men who died when the ship went down are inscribed on the wall. According to the memorial's architect, Alfred Preis, "The form, wherein the structure sags in the center but stands strong and vigorous at the ends, expresses initial defeat and ultimate victory."

The U.S. Navy was in charge of the memorial from 1962 to 1980. In March 1980 Congress turned its operation over to the National Park Service. The $5 million shoreside complex, which was completed in 1981, is operated by the National Park Service. It includes a visitor center with a museum, twin theaters, a bookstore, and a snack bar, in addition to the original shuttle boarding stalls. The U.S. Navy provides shuttle boat service to the memorial under an agreement with the National Park Service.

"Lots of people come out and lay flowers [at the Memorial Wall]. It's a sad time, but it's beautiful," says the woman sailor whose somber duty is running the shuttle boat.

The State Capitol

Hawai'i paid a huge price during World War II with the enormity of Pearl Harbor and the burden of years of martial law, not to mention the contributions of its people, particularly its distinguished all-Japanese 442nd Regiment. So it seemed that statehood would come quickly to the island territory. But Hawai'i was not admitted to the Union after the war, and arguments for and against statehood went on for years.

By the late 1950s, opposition had died down, and on March 12, 1959, the House of Representatives passed a bill conferring statehood on Hawai'i. It became official on August 21, 1959, when President Dwight D. Eisenhower read the proclamation declaring that Hawai'i had fulfilled all the requirements for statehood and was admitted to the Union.

'Iolani Palace, the territorial capitol, continued to serve as the state capitol until 1969. The government then moved to a new $24.5 million building, located directly behind the palace.

The State Capitol with its attractively landscaped grounds brings together elements from the islands' eventful passage into the modern world. The massive structure has a distinctively Hawaiian, open-air look, suggesting the state's oceanic and volcanic origins. In front of the building stands the powerful and disturbing bronze sculpture of Kalaupapa's Father Damien. The brooding, black figure created by sculptress Marisol Escobar shows the priest in the final stages

of his disease.

Two flags flutter in the tradewinds, the Star Spangled Banner and the state flag of Hawai'i. This red-white-and-blue flag bears the British Union Jack in the upper lefthand, a reminder of England's first contact with the ancient Hawaiian world through its emissary, Captain Cook. ■

► *Anthuriums, along with coffee, orchids, and macadamia nuts, is one of Hawai'i's familiar exports.*
WILLIAM WATERFALL

Where land and water meet

"Life's a beach."

Chapter five

The meeting of land and water—the beach—is Hawai'i's greatest recreational asset. There are 934 miles of tidal shoreline on the islands of Kaua'i, O'ahu, Moloka'i, Lāna'i, Maui, and Hawai'i, of which 185 miles (20 percent) is sandy beach. Less than 13 percent of the shoreline is considered well-suited for recreational purposes because of steeply sloping beaches, dangerous currents or surf, difficult access, or insufficient parking and other support facilities.

Beaches provide a different recreational experience for every beach-goer. For some, the object is to pursue the time-honored activity of relaxing, getting a tan (updated now with sunscreens), and people-watching. This activity has been elevated to a fine art at the parks fronting resort areas, such as Ala Moana, 'Aina Moana, Waikiki, Fort Derussy, and Kūhiō on O'ahu; the Kama'ole and Kā'anapali beaches on Maui; Po'ipū Beach on Kaua'i; and along the Kona coast of the Big Island.

More active beach-goers might throw footballs or frisbees, play volleyball or paddleball, or jog, as at Samuel M. Spencer Beach Park and Hāpuna State Recreation Area, also on the Big Island. Kualoa Regional Park on the windward shore of O'ahu offers a grassy area for volleyball, a beach that is part sand and part rocks, and a campground for those who need more than just a day of beach activities.

For the romance- or solitude-minded, walks along lonely stretches of sand and brilliantly colored sunsets give solace and satisfaction, as at Polihale State Park on Kaua'i. Fine sunsets can be viewed, in fact, from the southern and southwestern shores of all the islands.

Small children build sand castles, bury people, and dig holes (in this case to Africa, not China) at any sandy beach. After storms, beachcombers may find glass floats from Japanese fishing nets, shells, driftwood, and other treasures. Ocean currents toss particularly interesting things onto southern beaches.

At O'ahu's Mālaekahana State Recreation Area, feral cats commit feline crimes while campers set up their tents in wooded or grassy areas, cook at stone barbecues, swim, fish, nibble on salty sea grapes, or walk across the shallow channel to the bird sanctuary at Moku 'Auia. Less idyllic but close to the airport and downtown Honolulu, Sand Island State Recreation Area makes a convenient spot for a picnic or a base of operations for camping travelers who want to explore the city. Picnickers at Punalu'u Beach Park might eat gritty sandwiches and drink warmish beer amid hala and wispy ironwood trees. At Ala Moana and Kapi'olani parks, picnics can be held under the palm trees. When the sand gets too hot, swimming is a refreshing alternative.

While no beach is ever entirely safe, the safest are those protected by reefs or patrolled by lifeguards, who can point out rocky areas, rip currents, and other ocean hazards. From November to February, the northern shores are generally pounded by high surf. In the summer, storms from the

► Bathers explore the famous coral reef of Hanauma Bay State Underwater Park and relax on the sand at Hanauma Bay Beach Park on O'ahu. JEFF GNASS

► *Boogie boarding, left, is one of the many ways to enjoy the surf on Hawai'i's beaches.*
MICHAEL S. SAMPLE

► *Children, right, inspect the contents of a tidepool on Kaua'i.* AUDREY GIBSON

wintery southern hemisphere kick up waves on the south shores. Water conditions change from day to day and sometimes hour to hour. Living so close to the sea, early Hawaiians appreciated its many moods and learned the language of tides, currents, and waves. Today's uninitiated should listen to the surf reports on the radio and ask the lifeguard what to expect.

Among the many dangers of the ocean,

sharks are perhaps the most terrifying. There have been only two known shark-related deaths in Hawai'i since 1970, but this unpredictable predator demands respect in any event.

For people not content just to swim in the ocean, bodysurfing—the art of riding ocean waves using the body as the planing surface—can be a thrilling adjunct. One of the most dangerous

ocean activities, bodysurfing is much more difficult than it looks. Unwary practitioners get caught in rip currents or thrown to bottom, often sustaining serious injuries or drowning.

O'ahu has more bodysurfing beaches than any other island. The most hazardous—and the most popular—are Sandy and Makapu'u beaches. The Banzai Pipeline at Ehukai Beach Park is for

► *The sun, wind, and waves at Ho'okipa Beach, left, near Pā'ia on Maui are just right for sunbathing and boardsailing.*
DOUGLAS PEEBLES

► *A fisherman, right, leisurely awaits a strike at Barbers Point on O'ahu.* MICHAEL S. SAMPLE

experts only. Beginners should learn at the gentler breaks of Bellow's Field, "The Wall" at Waikiki, or the shorebreak at Hale'iwa Beach.

He'e nalu, or "wave sliding," now known as surfing, is Hawai'i's unique contribution to the world of recreation. The sport was more highly developed here than anywhere else in Polynesia. Ali'i paddled heavy, eighteen-foot koa wood

wood boards out into the surf, hoping then, as now, for the perfect wave. The missionaries discouraged surfing, probably because it looked like too much fun. Fortunately, the sport was revived, originally for its value to tourism, improved with new materials and hydrodynamically designed surfboards, and expanded. Today's international surfing championships are held at the same

O'ahu beaches—Sunset, Mākaha, Paumalū —that the ali'i used for their contests.

In a further enhancement of surfing, attaching a sail to a surfboard-like platform has resulted in boardsailing, or windsurfing. Practitioners find the combination of Hawai'i's waves and reliable tradewinds irresistible. Popular venues for either watching or participating in this colorful activity are

► *Lemon butterfly fish, right, flock to a diver at Molokini, off Maui.* ED ROBINSON/TOM STACK & ASSOCIATES

► *Slate-pencil urchins, far right, cling to coral and rocks.*
ED ROBINSON/TOM STACK & ASSOCIATES

Ho'okipa Park on Maui and Kailua Beach Park on O'ahu.

At some Hawaiian coastal parks, tidepools beckon. The volcanic coastline of Ka'ena Point State Park on O'ahu, for example, affords hours of exploration in tidepools that go on for miles. Chitons, limpets, sea cucumbers, hermit crabs, anemones, snails, small fish, and poisonous cone shells are some tidepool inhabitants. Reef tabis, felt-soled socks with a separate compartment for the big toe, give purchase on slippery surfaces and protect reef and tidepool explorers from

sea urchin spines, jagged rocks, and sharp coral.

'Opihi, a type of limpet, is considered a great delicacy by some residents of Hawai'i, who find them chewy and more flavorful than oysters or clams. Picking them is a traditional Hawaiian recreation, and for many people it represents a time to be with nature. The mollusks used to be much more widespread, but loss of habitat and pressure from pickers have reduced their numbers. This scarcity has turned a gentle pastime into an increasingly dangerous activity. Deter-mined pickers must now comb the wildest, most remote shores for 'opihi, and many people have been swept away by high surf or injured climbing down cliffs. Some 'opihi still cling to the rocks at Kalaupapa National Historical Park.

Hawai'i's warm, tropical waters and in-finitely varied communities of coral and colorful reef fish lure scuba divers and snorkelers. The state park system admin-isters two underwater parks, Kealakekua Bay on the Big Island and Hanauma Bay on O'ahu. At Kealakekua Bay, glass-bot-tom boats offer another way to view a relatively pristine underwater habitat.

Twenty minutes from Waikiki, snorkelers and divers at Hanauma Bay, a steep-sided volcanic crater open to the sea on one side, can observe a variety of fish, including parrotfish, surgeonfish, goatfish, and butterflyfish, corals, and other organisms. Because fishing restrictions were imposed here in 1967, the fish are quite tame. Some visitors chum the water with frozen green peas, which bring the fish flocking like pigeons to bread crumbs. For best viewing, the water in the bay should be turquoise. A greenish color

▶ *The Hawaiian lionfish, above, is venomous but reclusive and unaggressive. When provoked, the animal erects its venom-containing dorsal spines.*
BRIAN PARKER/TOM STACK & ASSOCIATES

means the water is turbid, with less visibility.

Except where restrictions apply, fishing is permitted year-round at almost every coastal park. People fish for pleasure and for subsistence, using a variety of methods. At Ka'a'awa Beach Park on O'ahu, for example, fishermen go "squidding" for octopus (using a spear), throw-net fishing for moi and manini (typical reef fish), and surf fishing for papio (small ulua under ten pounds), with light bait-casting tackle. At night fishermen continue the Hawaiian tradition of torch fishing, now luring fish to the light of a lantern instead of a kukui nut torch.

Even the most dedicated beach-goer will find hiking in a lush forest among trees—some familiar, some exotic, some distinctly Hawaiian—a rewarding experience.

Just as the ocean has its hazards, the mountains of Hawai'i call for respect and caution as well. Some are noted for their loose rocks and overgrown volcanic cracks, and abundant rainfall makes windward trails slick and muddy. Dangerous flash flooding occurs in some gulches, and above 7,000 feet hypothermia can be an unexpected problem. Wear appropriate footgear to protect your feet from jagged lava rocks and sharp kiawe thorns that can tear flipflops and sneakers to shreds. Large centipedes (up to eight inches) may crawl into empty hiking boots and inflict a painful bite when you reintroduce your foot. Carry drinking water, and clean your boots thoroughly to prevent the spread of

▶ *A two-mile hike leads to the base of the eighty-foot waterfall at Sacred Falls State Park on O'ahu. The trail is closed during rainy weather.* DAVID MUENCH

noxious plant species, such as *Clidemia,* from place to place and island to island. In backcountry areas, stay on the main trails to avoid conflicts with marijuana growers.

Some hikers plan their outings according to the seasonal ripening of fruit, which may be picked on public lands for personal consumption. Plums attract visitors to Kōke'e and Kahana Valley state parks and Polipoli Spring State Recreation Area. Guavas grow almost everywhere. Thimbleberries, raspberries, blackberries, 'ōhelo berries, strawberries, mangoes, and papayas are some of the other fruits to enjoy.

Hawai'i has more than a thousand miles of trails—most of them not maintained— and many excellent guidebooks to them are available. Also, groups such as the Sierra Club, Hawai'i Trail and Mountain Club, Friends of Foster Garden, and Moanalua Garden Foundation sponsor organized hikes, which are listed in local newspapers.

The Big Island, because of its geologic youth, size, and geographic diversity, offers some of the finest hiking trails in the state. Hawai'i Volcanoes National Park has excellent hiking and camping opportunities with its Mauna Loa and Ka'ū Desert trails. Kalōpā State Recreation Area has an easy family nature trail in a native 'ōhi'a forest, access to hiking trails in the nearby forest reserve, and facilities for camping.

Treks into Haleakalā National Park offer escape from what many people consider to be an overdeveloped Maui. Or, close

► *Hikers traverse the Kalalau Trail in Nā Pali Coast State Park.*
ED COOPER

► *The cool mountain air of Kaua'i's Kōke'e State Park attracts visitors to its campgrounds.* GREG VAUGHN

► *A backcountry hiker, right, stops to stretch en route to a cabin on the floor of the Halekalā Crater.* BOB KIESLING

to the ocean, you can enjoy solitude, hiking, and camping at Wai'ānapanapa State Park.

Moloka'i has no official trails except at Pālā'au State Park; Lāna'i has none.

On O'ahu, in the mountains above Pearl Harbor, Keaīwa Heiau State Recreation Area features the 4.8-mile 'Aiea loop trail, which provides a chance to see native 'ōhi'a and koa trees. Rustic facilities for camping and picnicking are available. Other places to hike include Diamond Head State Monument and Sacred Falls, Ka'ena Point, and Kahana Valley state parks.

Kōke'e State Park on Kaua'i has about

forty-five miles of hiking trails. For wilderness hiking and primitive camping on the beach, Nā Pali Coast State Park is a magnificent resource.

Camping facilities at state parks range from primitive campgrounds with pit toilets and sometimes piped, but undrinkable, water to comfortable, fully equipped housekeeping cabins. In between are developed campgrounds with tables, barbecue grills, piped water, restrooms, dressing rooms, cold showers, paved roads, and parking lots. Some campgrounds have A-frame shelters, which consist of a single room with a wooden sleeping platform and a picnic

table. Shelter users share a centrally located pavilion with a range, refrigerator, tables, cold showers, and restrooms.

Housekeeping cabins have a kitchen-living room, a bathroom, and one to three bedrooms. Each unit is completely furnished with bedroom and kitchen furniture, electric range, refrigerator, hot shower, bathroom, bedding, linen, towels, dishes, and cooking and eating utensils. In cold mountain areas, fireplaces or electric heat provide warmth. Polipoli Spring State Recreation Area on Maui has no electricity or refrigerators, but gas lanterns provide illumination. Trailer campers are permitted only at Kōke'e and Polihale state parks on Kaua'i. Permits are required for camping, and the state charges a fee for the use of shelters and cabins.

State park picnic facilities have tables or shelters, barbecue grills, drinking water, restrooms, pavilions, paved roads, and parking lots. Beach parks may also have cold showers and dressing rooms.

Haleakalā and Hawai'i Volcanoes national parks have campgrounds, some with cabins, and primitive cabins accessible only by trail. Hawai'i Volcanoes also offers hotel accommodations at Volcano House.

County parks generally have more modest facilities than the state and national parks, and permits are required for their use. Lāna'i has no public camping facilities, but there is a private campground. Moloka'i has camping at Pālā'au State Park and at private campgrounds as well. See the directory for more information.

Sportsmen usually don't think of Hawai'i for hunting and fishing (except deep sea fishing). But the state boasts sixteen species of game birds, fifteen with open seasons; seven species of game animals, six with open seasons; and many species of freshwater fish. The Polynesians brought pigs to the islands, and sea captains brought other animals in order to have supplies of fresh meat available on future visits. Later, sportsmen released game birds, mammals, and fish.

While most hunting takes place in the forest reserves or on private lands, people also hunt at some of the parks, helping to reduce the damage caused by feral pigs, sheep, and goats. Kōke'e, Nā Pali, and Waimea Canyon state parks on Kaua'i permit hunting of deer, pigs, and goats. Kahana Valley State Park on O'ahu has pig hunting, Polipoli Spring State Recreation Area on Maui has pig and upland bird hunting, and Mauna Kea State Recreation Area permits hunting of pigs, sheep, and upland birds nearby. Information about hunting can be obtained from the state Division of Forestry and Wildlife.

In addition to feral pigs, sheep, and goats, other big game species include axis deer, a spotted deer native to India and Sri Lanka (found on Moloka'i and Lāna'i), black-tailed deer (Kaua'i), and mouflon sheep, also called European bighorn sheep (Lāna'i and the Big Island).

Upland game bird species available are: ring-necked pheasant, green pheasant, Kalij pheasant (found on the Big Island only), gray francolin, black francolin, Erkel's francolin, chukar, California quail,

▶ *The axis deer, an introduced game animal found on Lāna'i and Moloka'i, retains its white-spotted coat in all seasons and at all ages.* GREG VAUGHN

► *Tour boats ply the Wailua River, left, the islands' only navigable river, in Kaua'i's Wailua River State Park.* ED COOPER

► *From the 13,796-foot summit of Mauna Kea, far left, the rising sun appears to be embedded in the clouds.* PHIL DEGGINGER

Gambel's quail (Lāna'i only), Japanese quail, chestnut-bellied sand grouse (Big Island only), mourning dove (Big Island only), spotted dove, zebra dove, and wild turkey. Closed to hunting are pronghorn, feral cattle, rock wallaby, Barbary partridge, and rock dove. All ducks, geese, and other waterbirds in the state are closed to hunting.

On Kaua'i, anglers fish for rainbow trout in Kōke'e and Waimea Canyon state parks during an annual open season and for smallmouth bass in Wailua River State Park. On O'ahu, Wahiawā Freshwater

State Recreation Area has 300 acres of fishable water containing largemouth bass; bluegill sunfish; smallmouth bass; channel catfish; tilapia, a bluegill look-alike native to Africa; snakehead, or pongee, an eel-like fish native to Asia; carp; Chinese catfish, or puntat, native to the lowlands of southern China, Malaya, and India; tucunare, a popular game fish introduced from British Guiana; and oscar, the familiar aquarium fish, a good fighter native to South America. Wahiawā offers year-round shore and boat fishing but no swimming or water skiing.

On the Big Island, Wailoa River State Recreation Area in downtown Hilo features Waiākea Pond, a twenty-six-acre, spring-fed estuary supporting a variety of brackish and saltwater species.

If Hawai'i doesn't come to mind for hunting and fishing, it may seem even less likely for skiing. Yet snow suitable for skiing regularly accumulates on the upper slopes of 13,796-foot Mauna Kea between December and May. Mauna Kea State Recreation Area, with heated housekeeping cabins, serves as a convenient base of operations for skiers.

With only forty miles of designated bikeways, bicyclists must generally share the roads with vehicular traffic. Maui presents the greatest bike challenge in all Hawai'i—the ride to the top of Haleakalā. Considered by many to be the hardest ride in the world, the road rises more than 10,000 feet in just forty miles. Easier by far is renting a bicycle, being driven to the top, and descending.

Another beautiful bike ride on Maui is the Hana Highway, with frequent stops at the state waysides, to Wai'ānapanapa State Park, Hana, and 'O'heo Gulch. The

► *The slopes of Mauna Kea accommodate beginning to expert skiers.* GREG VAUGHN

►*Hawai'i Volcanoes National Park hosts the annual Kīlauea Volcano Marathon and Rim Runs.* GREG VAUGHN

road winds tortuously and has narrow shoulders and very heavy traffic, so cyclists should be very cautious.

Horseback riding is a pleasant way to sightsee in the crater of Haleakalā, and two private companies lead tours here. Stables are found on all the islands, but few parks have bridle paths. Kalōpā State Recreation Area on the Big Island is one that offers a two-mile loop trail for equestrians.

A famous launch site for hang gliders is the ''Green Wall,'' the near-vertical sea cliff behind Makapu'u Beach Park on windward O'ahu. The tradewinds, which flow unobstructed across the Pacific, provide the hang glider with a smooth and steady stream of air that permits him to launch his craft with a minimum of effort and keep it aloft for hours. Thermals rising off lava fields are another source of lift for the delicate aircraft.

Hawai'i is said to have the greatest number of runners per capita in the United States, or about ten times the national average. To meet their competitive needs, Hawai'i offers several organized challenges. The Honolulu Marathon, held annually in December, has grown from 162 starters in 1973 to more than 7,500 in 1987. The race course goes from Waikiki to Kapi'olani Park, around Diamond Head, circles the housing development of Hawai'i Kai, then reverses the route to finish at Kapi'olani Park.

At Hawai'i Volcanoes National Park, the annual Kīlauea Volcano Marathon and Rim Runs physically and mentally challenge the hardiest runners. Founded in 1983, the January races benefit cultural programs at the Volcano Art Center, a gallery and cultural center located inside the park. Marathoners run in and out of Kīlauea and then head for the Kaʻū Desert. The rim runs, a ten-mile and a 5.5-mile race, skirt the crater.

The Ironman World Triathlon Championship takes place on the Big Island as well, with swimming, bicycling, and running on the Kona Coast. Held each year in October, the competition attracts more than a thousand entrants. The first leg is a 2.4-mile swim in Kailua Bay. The bicycling leg takes cyclists from Kailua-Kona to Hāwi at the northern tip of the island and back, a grueling 112 miles. For the third leg, marathoners start at the Kona Surf Resort, run to the Old Kona Airport State Recreation Area, and finish in Kailua-Kona—a distance of 26.2 miles

Hawaiʻi has many recreational possibilities, with new ones being invented and old ones revived or updated. One pastime that would be hard to improve upon is sightseeing. Many parks in Hawaiʻi preserve scenic treasures or offer vantage points from which to enjoy superb views of the landscape. Much is worth preserving in photographs.

On Kauaʻi, these parks are Kōkeʻe, for

▶ *Kapiʻolani Park offers a wide range of diversions, from an archery field to the Honolulu Zoo. These visitors have chosen simply to relax at the end of a long day.* ED COOPER

▶ *Legend says that the cave beneath eighty-foot Rainbow Falls in Hilo's Wailuku River State Park was the home of Hina, mother of the demigod Maui.* JEFF GNASS

its spectacular views of Niʻihau and the Nā Pali Coast; Waimea Canyon, with its rugged Grand Canyonesque features; and Wailua River, for its vistas of the river valley and waterfalls.

The view of windward Oʻahu from Nuʻuanu Pali State Wayside is unforgettable. Visitors to Puʻu Ualakaʻa State Wayside never tire of the panoramic view of Honolulu and Diamond Head from Round Top. Sand Island State Recreation Area gives a different perspective on the cityscape with its view looking into Honolulu Harbor. Waʻahila Ridge State Recreation Area features yet another angle on Honolulu with its views of Mānoa and Pālolo valleys.

Molokaʻi's Pālāʻau State Park permits viewing of the Kalaupapa Peninsula, while on Maui, Kaumahina State Wayside offers a vista of that island's low-cliffed, northeastern coast. Observers at Wailua Valley State Wayside see the windward side of Haleakalā, picturesque taro patches, and the endless Pacific. The needle at ʻIao Valley State Monument always demands a photograph. On the Big Island, the 442-foot waterfall at ʻAkaka Falls State Park draws visitors, as do eighty-foot Rainbow Falls and other viewpoints at Wailuku River State Park in Hilo.

Hawaiʻi's parklands are, indeed, recreational treasures, offering a range of diversions unequaled in the United States. Many of their resources are well-developed for residents and visitors, and others await the imaginations of future planners and inventive recreation seekers. ■

▶ *Night falls at Nu'uanu Pali State Wayside on O'ahu.*
B. BRENT BLACK

Chapter six

In closing

The public parks of Hawai'i, of which there are almost 700, fall under federal, state, and county jurisdiction. Seven national parks, encompassing 294,224 acres, preserve natural and historic areas of outstanding national significance. Sixty-seven state parks, with nearly 25,000 acres, preserve scenic, cultural, historical, and recreational sites. Approximately 8,187 acres in 617 county parks, usually beach parks or parks within population centers, provide for local recreation.

The oldest park in the islands is Thomas Square in Honolulu, set aside by King Kamehameha IV in 1843 (twenty-nine years before Yellowstone National Park was established). The newest may be Kaloko Honokōhau National Historical Park on the Kona coast of the Big Island.

In the state system, the most frequently visited parks are Kahana Valley State Park and Nu'uanu Pali State Wayside on O'ahu; 'Īao Valley State Monument on Maui; Wailua River, Kōke'e, and Waimea Canyon state parks on Kaua'i; and Wailuku River and Hāpuna Beach state recreation areas and 'Akaka Falls State Park on the Big Island.

Combined with the million and a half acres of unimproved forest and hunting lands and the acreage of the national wildlife refuges, Hawai'i has close to two million acres of public outdoor and open space. But land in Hawai'i is limited, and developers, agriculturists, and others compete fiercely for it. More than any other state, Hawai'i, isolated in the middle of the Pacific with a growing population and expanding tourist economy, needs its parklands.

Hawai'i's unique ecology is its most fragile—and its most threatened—resource. At Hawai'i Volcanoes National Park, for example, there are a dozen or so special ecological areas, from which nonnative species have been eradicated. The National Park Service can't save the whole park, but they can at least reserve scattered portions of it for native plants and animals. In the national wildlife refuges, the U.S. Fish and Wildlife Service is dedicated to preserving and restoring native habitat for native species. The state's system of natural area reserves protects more than 100,000 acres of forests, bogs, grasslands, dunes, and other disappearing ecosystems. Private organizations, such as The Nature Conservancy and the Trust for Public Land, acquire sensitive lands necessary for the continuation of some of Hawai'i's endangered wildlife. But even these measures are not adequate.

Exotic plants have already taken over much of Hawai'i's parklands, and in many areas controlling feral animals is too expensive, impractical, or unpopular. Irresponsible people do unthinking damage to the environment. Through education, residents and visitors can come to a deeper awareness of the problems facing native Hawai'i and work toward fulfilling the state motto: "The life of the land is perpetuated in righteousness."

In preserving archaeological sites, many parks contribute to the understanding, appreciation, and

► *A master surfer rides one of the many big waves that makes the Pipeline on O'ahu famous.*
GARY HOFHEIMER

enjoyment of native Hawaiian heritage. Parks such as Lapakahi State Historical Park and Pu'uhonua o Hōnaunau on the Big Island help preserve the fabric of Hawaiian culture with historical restorations and demonstrations of traditional activities. The fact that efforts are being made to restore the natural environment in these parks adds to the authenticity and pleasure of visiting them.

The attempt to preserve traditional Hawaiian values at Kahana Valley State Park on O'ahu might be somewhat impractical, but the goal is worth pursuing. Hawaiian culture has contributed greatly to our human heritage. Compatibility with the natural environment, tolerance of racial diversity, and the ineffable spirit of aloha—warmth, friendliness, respect, and hospitality—are all Hawaiian qualities. Only a few parks emphasize Hawaiian culture, and more should be established because not all residents have opportunities for interisland travel. Many tourists see only one or two islands.

Some aspects of Hawaiian history after

European contact are well-preserved and interpreted in the parks. 'Iolani Palace State Monument and the U.S.S. *Arizona* Memorial are striking examples. However, many gaps exist in the historical record as it is kept in the parks. Traces of whaling, the sugarcane industry, the social history of immigrants, to name the obvious omissions, are stored in museums, in the restorations of historical societies, and informally on the streets of the cities and towns, but not in the parks.

Greater efforts at interpretation would enhance the value of Hawai'i's parklands and, in a place where land resources are scarce, make them go further. Parks are an antidote to overdevelopment, their attractions draw tourists who promote the economy, and they provide vital recreational outlets for residents. Visiting the parks of Hawai'i expands the horizons of people throughout the state, the nation, and beyond. In many ways, the parklands of Hawai'i are an underdeveloped resource. ■

▶ *A favorite spot for sightseers, the Fern Grotto in Wailua River State Park gives the visitor a rare opportunity to enjoy the atmosphere of a tropical jungle setting.* ED COOPER

▶ *At Ka'ena Point State Park on O'ahu, the rocks bear witness to the timeless interplay of sea and land.* MICHAEL S. SAMPLE

Hawai'i parklands directory

ISLAND OF HAWAI'I

FEDERAL PARKLANDS

Hakalau Forest National Wildlife Refuge

c/o Hawaiian and Pacific Islands NWRs
P.O. Box 50167 or 300 Ala Moana Blvd.
Honolulu, HI 96850
(808) 541-1201

About 12 miles northwest of Hilo on Keanakolu Rd. off Hwy. 200 (Saddle Rd.). Entry by special permit from refuge manager. Mid-elevation mesic and wet forest. Endangered 'akiapōla-'au, 'akepa, Hawai'i creeper, Hawaiian hawk, 'o'u, Hawaiian hoary bat.

Hawai'i Volcanoes National Park

Hawai'i National Park, HI 96718
(808) 967-7311

30 miles southwest of Hilo on Hwy. 11. Active volcanoes. Backcountry camping (registration required, shelters and cabins), tent and trailer camping, hiking, scenic driving with lookouts. Art center, hotel, museum, visitor center. Wheelchair-accessible areas, parking, restrooms. Hunting, trapping, collecting rocks and plants prohibited. Entrance fee.

Kaloko Honokōhau National Historical Park

c/o Pu'uhonua o Hōnaunau,
P.O. Box 129
Hōnaunau, HI 96726
(808) 328-2326

3 miles north of Kailua-Kona on Queen Ka'ahumanu Hwy. (Hwy.19). Currently 350 acres. Viewing historical Hawaiian site. Open 7:30 a.m. to 4:00 p.m. Guided tours by appointment. Under development.

Pu'uhonua o Hōnaunau
National Historic Park

P.O. Box 129
Hōnaunau, HI 96726
(808) 328-2326

19 miles south of Kailua off Hwy. 160 near Hōnaunau. 180 acres. Sanctuary established in 15th century. Cultural demonstrations, picnicking, self-guided walking tour, orientation talks. Visitor center. Wheechair-accessible area, parking, restrooms, phone. Entrance fee.

Pu'ukoholā Heiau National Historic Site

P.O. Box 4963
Kawaihae, HI 96743
(808) 882-7218

A mile south of Kawaihae off Hwy. 270. 77 acres. Last-built major religious structure of the ancient Hawaiians. Self-guided tour; picnicking and swimming at Spencer Beach Park. Visitor center.

STATE PARKLANDS

Division of State Parks, Hawai'i District
P.O. Box 936 or 75 Aupuni St.
Hilo, HI 96721-0936
(808) 961-7200
Permit required for camping.

'Akaka Falls State Park

3.6 miles southwest of Honomū, at end of 'Akaka Falls Rd. (Hwy. 220). 65.4 acres. Lush tropical vegetation. Hiking, scenic viewing.

Hāpuna Beach State Recreation Area

2.3 miles south of Kawaihae on Queen Ka'ahumanu Hwy. (Hwy. 19). 61.1 acres. Landscaped beach park. Camping (shelters, fee), pole fishing, picnicking, scuba diving, snorkeling, expert surfing, bodyboarding, and bodysurfing, swimming when calm. Pavilions, restrooms, showers. Wheelchair-accessible area, restroom, phone on upper level.

Kalōpā State Recreation Area

5 miles southeast of Honoka'a, at end of Kalōpā Rd., 3 miles inland from Hwy. 19. 100 acres. Native 'ohi'a forest. Camping (permit required), easy family hiking, picnicking. Group lodging (fee), pavilion. Wheelchair-accessible picnic area.

Kamehameha I Birthsite State Monument

1.6 miles southwest of 'Upolu airport, on dirt road off 'Upolu Airport Rd. from Hwy. 270. 0.5 acre. Memorial to Hawaiian king. Wheelchair accessible.

Kealakekua Bay State Historical Park

In Nāpo'opo'o, at end of Beach Rd. off Government Rd. from Hwy. 160. 0.8 acre. Scenic viewing of site of worship of Captain Cook/Lono.

Kealakekua Bay State Underwater Park

Access from Nāpo'opo'o Beach at end of Beach Rd. off Government Rd. from Hwy. 160. 315 acres. Sandy and rocky beach. Boating, fishing, picnicking, snorkeling, scuba diving, swimming. Commercial glass-bottom boat tours. Restrooms, showers.

Kīlauea State Recreation Area

29 miles south of Hilo on Hwy. 11. 7.3 acres. 'Ōhi'a and fern forest. One housekeeping cabin (fee).

Lapakahi State Historical Park

12 miles north of Kawaihae on Hwy. 270. 262 acres. Re-enactment of early Hawaiian life; shoreline is marine life conservation district. Rocky beach. Scuba diving, snorkeling, swimming, self-guided walking tour. Restrooms.

Lava Tree State Monument

2.7 miles southeast of Pāhoa off Hwy. 132. 17 acres. Lava tree forest. Picnicking, scenic viewing. No drinking water.

MacKenzie State Recreation Area

9 miles northeast of Kaimū on Hwy. 137. 13.1 acres. Wild volcanic coastline. Shore fishing, tent camping (permit required), hiking, picnicking. No drinking water.

Manukā State Wayside

19.3 miles west of Nā'ālehu on Hwy. 11. 13.4 acres. Camping (permit required, shelters), picnicking. Pavilion. Wheelchair-accessible picnic area. No drinking water.

Mauna Kea State Recreation Area

35.1 miles west of Hilo on Hwy. 200. 20 acres. Disruptive periodic military maneuvers. Picnicking, nearby pig/sheep/bird hunting. Cabins (fee).

Mo'okini Heiau State Monument

1.6 miles southwest of 'Upolu airport on dirt road off Airport Rd. from Hwy. 270. 3.2 acres. National historic landmark. Scenic viewing.

Old Kona Airport State Recreation Area

0.8 mile north of Kailua Pier at end of Hwy. 11. 117.8 acres. Sand and rock coastline. Shore and spear fishing, picnicking, scuba diving, snorkeling, bodyboarding, bodysurfing, surfing, tidepooling, wading. Athletic fields, pavilions, restrooms, showers, tennis courts.

Wailoa River State Recreation Area

Downtown Hilo, at end of Pi'ilani St. 149.6 acres. Landscaped park, spring-fed estuary. Boat fishing (restrictions), picnicking, pleasure walking. Boat ramp, pavilion, visitor center. Wheelchair-accessible area, parking, restrooms.

Wailuku River State Park

In Hilo off Waiānuenue Ave. 16.3 acres. Basalt lava pools, falls. Scenic viewing.

COUNTY PARKLANDS

Hawai'i County Dept. of Parks & Recreation
25 Aupuni St.
Hilo, HI 96720
(808) 961-8311
Permit required for camping, fee charged.

H.K. Brown Beach Park

30 miles south of Hilo off Hwy. 130 at Kalapana. Camping, fishing, picnicking, snorkeling, swimming. Pavilions, restrooms, showers. Wheelchair accessible.

Carlsmith Park

3 miles east of downtown Hilo off Kalaniana'ole Ave., at Keaukaha. Picnicking, fishing, snorkeling, swimming. Pavilions, restrooms, showers.

Glenwood Park

16 miles southwest of Hilo off Hwy. 11 at Glenwood. Picnicking. Pavilions, restrooms.

Isaac Hale Beach Park

8 miles southeast of Pāhoa off Hwy. 132 at Pohoiki. Camping, fishing, picnicking, snorkeling, swimming. Pavilions, restrooms. No drinking water.

Ho'okena Beach Park

24 miles south of Kailua off Hwy. 11 at Ho'okena. Fishing, picnicking, snorkeling, swimming. Pavilions, restrooms, showers.

No drinking water.

Kahalu'u Beach Park

6 miles south of Kailua on Ali'i Dr. at Kahalu'u. Sandy beach. Fishing, picnicking, scuba diving, snorkeling, bodyboarding, surfing, swimming. Pavilions, restrooms, showers.

Kaimū (Black Sand) Beach

30 miles south of Hilo off Hwy. 130 at Kalapana. Fishing, picnicking. No drinking water.

Kapa'a Beach Park

32 miles northwest of Waimea off Hwy. 270. Camping, fishing, picnicking, snorkeling, swimming. Pavilions, restrooms, showers. No drinking water.

Kaūmana Caves

5 miles west of downtown Hilo off Kaūmana Dr. Picnicking. Pavilions, restrooms.

James Kealoha Beach Park

4 miles from downtown Hilo on Kalaniana'ole Ave. Rocky beach. Camping, fishing, picnicking, snorkeling, strolling, bodyboarding, surfing, swimming. Lifeguard, restrooms, showers.

Keōkea Beach Park

27 miles north of Waimea off Hwy. 250 at Niuli'i. Camping, fishing, picnicking. Pavilions, restrooms, showers.

Kolekole Beach Park

13 miles north of Hilo off Hwy. 19 at Wailea. Camping, fishing, picnicking. Pavilions, restrooms, showers. No drinking water.

Laupāhoehoe Beach Park

25 miles north of Hilo off Hwy. 19 at Laupāhoehoe. Camping, fishing, picnicking. Pavilions, restrooms, showers.

Leleiwi Beach Park

5 miles east of downtown Hilo on Kalaniana'ole Ave. Fishing, picnicking, snorkeling, swimming. Pavilions, restrooms, showers.

Lili'uokalani Gardens

1 mile north of downtown Hilo off Manono St. Picnicking. Pavilions, restrooms.

Magic (Disappearing) Sands Beach

5 miles south of Kailua on Ali'i Drive. Restrooms, showers.

Māhukona Beach Park

30 miles northwest of Waimea off Hwy. 270 at Māhukona. Rocky beach, interpretive display. Camping, picnicking (tables), scuba diving, snorkeling, sunbathing, swimming. Lifeguards, pavilions, restrooms, showers. No drinking water.

Miloli'i Beach Park

25 miles south of Hōnaunau off Hwy. 11 at Miloli'i. Camping, fishing, picnicking, snorkeling, swimming. Restrooms. Wheelchair accessible. No drinking water.

Nāpo'opo'o Beach Park

13 miles south of Kailua off Hwy. 11 at Nāpo'opo'o. Picnicking. Pavilions, restrooms, showers.

Onekahakaha Beach Park

3.5 miles east of downtown Hilo off Kalaniana'ole Ave. Sandy and rocky beach. Protected, shallow ocean pool for young children. Camping, fishing, picnicking, snorkeling, swimming, wading. Lifeguard, pavilions, restrooms, showers. Wheelchair-accessible area, restroom, phone.

Punalu'u Beach Park

48 miles south of Hilo off Hwy. 11 at Punalu'u. Camping, fishing, picnicking. Pavilions, restrooms, showers.

Reeds Bay Beach Park

2 miles southeast of downtown Hilo off Kalaniana'ole Ave. Fishing, picnicking, snorkeling, swimming. Restrooms, showers.

Richardson Ocean Park

5 miles east of downtown Hilo on Kalaniana'ole Ave. Sandy beach. Fishing, picnicking, snorkeling, sunbathing, bodyboarding, surfing, swimming. Pavilions, restrooms, showers. Wheelchair accessible.

Spencer Beach Park

27 miles north of Keāhole airport, off Hwy. 270. Sandy beach, good for young children. Camping, fishing, picnicking, scuba diving, snorkeling, swimming. Pavilions, restrooms, showers, tennis courts. Wheelchair-accessible picnic area, phone.

Waikaumalo Park

18 miles north of Hilo off Hwy. 19 at Honohina. Picnicking. Pavilions, restrooms.

Wai'ōhinu Park

58 miles south of Hilo off Hwy. 11 at Wai'ōhinu. Picnicking. Pavilions, restrooms.

Waipi'o Valley Lookout

49 miles north of Hilo via Hwy. 19 to end of Hwy. 240 at Kukuihaele. Picnicking. Pavilions, restrooms. No drinking water.

Whittington Beach Park

53 miles south of Hilo off Hwy. 11 at Honu'apo. Camping, fishing, picnicking. Pavilions, restrooms, showers. No drinking water.

OTHER PARKLANDS

'Ahu'ena Heiau

c/o Hotel King Kamehameha
75-5660 Palani Rd.
Kailua-Kona, HI 96740
(808) 329-2911

On hotel grounds near fishing boat docks. Replica of King Kamehameha's final royal residence. Historical walking tours.

'Anaeho'omalu Beach

At Sheraton Royal Waikoloa Hotel, 26 miles north of Kailua-Kona off Hwy. 19. Public access, sandy beach. Picnicking, sailing, scuba diving, snorkeling, bodyboarding, surfing, wind surfing, swimming. Restrooms, showers, equipment rental, water-sport instruction (fee).

Hawai'i Tropical Botanical Garden

P.O. Box 1415
Hilo, HI 96721
(808) 964-5233

7 miles north of Hilo off Hwy. 19 at Onomea Bay. 17 acres. Nonprofit foundation nature preserve protecting tropical rain forest. Self-guided trail. Entrance fee.

Hōnaunau Bay

Next to Pu'uhonua o Hōnaunau National Historical Park, 19 miles south of Kailua off Hwy. 160. Rocky beach, humpback-whale sightings possible in winter. Scuba diving, snorkeling, swimming. Boat ramp, restrooms.

Waipi'o Valley

49 miles north of Hilo via Hwy. 19 to end of Hwy. 240 at Kukuihaele. Take privately owned, steep, 4-wheel-drive-only road to valley floor and black sand beach. Roads and beach area are generally considered public-accessible areas.

ISLAND OF MAUI

FEDERAL PARKLANDS

Haleakalā National Park

P.O. Box 369
Makawao, HI 96768
(808) 572-9306

37 miles (2 hrs.) out of Kahului, following Hwys. 36, 37, 377, and 378 sequentially, to visitor center. 'Ohe'o Gulch on the Kipahulu side is 62 miles (3 hrs.) out of Kahului via Hwys. 36, 360, and 31. 28,000 acres. Camping (permit required at crater sites), hiking, horseback riding, nature study, picnicking, scenic drives, overlooks, swimming. Cabins in crater by reservation. Wheelchair-accessible entrance, visitor center, parking.

STATE PARKLANDS

Division of State Parks, Maui Dist.
P.O. Box 1049 or 54 High St.
Wailuku, HI 96793
(808) 244-4354
Permit required for camping.

Division of Forestry & Wildlife,
Maui Dist.
P.O. Box 1015 or 54 High St.
Wailuku, HI 96793
(808) 244-4352

Haipua'ena Recreation Site

About 27 miles east of Kahului airport off Hana Hwy. (Hwy. 360). Hiking, risky wading and swimming (flash floods). No drinking water or restrooms. (Contact Div. of Forestry and Wildlife.)

Haleki'i-Pihana Heiau State Monument

In Wailuku, at end of Hea Place off Kūhiō Place from Wai'ehu Beach Rd. (Hwy. 340). 10.2 acres. Remains of two important heiau. Viewing of central Maui. No drinking water.

'Īao Valley State Monument

4 miles west of Wailuku at end of 'Īao Valley Road (Hwy. 320). 6.2 acres. Botanical garden, scenic viewing of 'Īao Needle, an

erosional feature which rises abruptly 1,200 feet from valley floor. Swimming (natural pools). Restrooms, shelters. Wheelchair-accessible entrance, parking, restrooms.

Kanaha Bird Sanctuary

1.5 miles southwest of Kahului airport at jct. Hwys. 36 and 37. Observation hut. (Contact Div. of Forestry and Wildlife.)

Kaumahina State Wayside

28 miles (2 hours) east of Kahului Airport on Hana Hwy. (Hwy. 360). 7.8 acres. Forested rest stop, showy exotic plants. Camping (no showers), picnic tables, scenic viewing. Restrooms, grills.

Ke'anae Arboretum

About 35 miles east of Kahului airport, entrance on sharp turn of Hwy. 360 between YMCA Camp Ke'anae and turnoff to Ke'anae village. Native and introduced plants in old-Hawaii cultural setting. Hiking (boots recommended), risky wading and swimming (flash floods). No drinking water or restrooms. (Contact Div. of Forestry and Wildlife.)

Launiupoko State Wayside

On west coast, 3 miles south of Lahaina on Hono-a-Pi'ilani Hwy. (Hwy. 30). 5.7 acres. Small beach park. Fishing, picnicking (tables), seaweed and shell collecting, swimming. Restrooms, children's wading pool, grills.

Pāpalaua State Wayside

14 miles southwest of Kahului Airport on Hono-a-Pi'ilani Hwy. (Hwy. 30). 6.7 acres. Small wooded beach park. Fishing, picnicking (tables), snorkeling, swimming. No drinking water.

Polipoli Spring State Recreation Area

9.7 miles south of Kula on Waipoli Road off Hwy. 377 in Kula Forest Reserve. 10 acres. 4-wheel drive advised. Tent camping (no showers), hiking, picnicking (tables), scenic viewing, pig and seasonal bird hunting. Restrooms, grills. One cabin (fee, no electricity, gas lanterns).

Pua'a Ka'a State Wayside

38 miles (2.5 hours) east of Kahului Airport on Hana Hwy. (Hwy. 360). Rain forest. Picnicking (tables), scenic viewing, swimming (natural pools). Restrooms, grills, shelters. Wheelchair-accessible area and restrooms.

Puohokamoa Recreation Site

About 28 miles east of Kahului airport off Hana Hwy. (Hwy. 360).

Tropical plants. Hiking, picnicking (table, shelter), risky wading and swimming (flash floods). No drinking water or restrooms. (Contact Div. of Forestry and Wildlife.)

Wahikuli State Wayside

2.5 miles north of Lahaina on Hono-a-Pi'ilani Hwy. (Hwy. 30). 8.3 acres. Small beach park. Canoeing, fishing, picnicking (shelters), some bodysurfing. Restrooms, outdoor shower, stoves.

Wai'anapanapa State Park

52.8 miles (3 hours) east of Kahului Airport off Hana Hwy. (Hwy. 360). 120 acres. Remote volcanic coastline, heiau, caves. Birdwatching, tent and trailer camping, fishing, hardy family hiking, picnicking (tables), scenic viewing, swimming. Restrooms, outdoor showers and stoves, cabins (fee). Wheelchair-accessible area.

Waikamoi Recreation Site

26 miles east of Kahului airport off Hana Hwy. (Hwy. 360). Hiking, risky wading and swimming (flash floods). Springwater drinking fountain. No restrooms. (Contact Div. of Forestry and Wildlife.)

Wailua Valley State Wayside

34 miles (2.25 hours) east of Kahului Airport on Hana Hwy. (Hwy. 360). 1.5 acres. Scenic viewing. No drinking water.

COUNTY PARKLANDS

County Parks Department
War Memorial Center
Wailuku, HI 96793
(808) 244-9018
Permit required for camping.

Baldwin Park

About 7 miles east of Kahului airport on Hana Hwy. (Hwy. 360). Windward shore. Tent camping (fee), picnicking (tables), scenic viewing, swimming. Restrooms, shelters. Wheelchair-accessible area.

Fleming Beach Park

About 9 miles north of Lahaina off Hwy. 30. Sheltered bay. Picnicking (tables), swimming. Restrooms, grills, shelters.

Hana Beach Park

52 miles east of Kahului on Hwy. 360, at Hana. Remnants of Hana Bay Pier and short walk to Queen Ka'ahumanu birthplace near lighthouse. Picnicking. Restrooms, grills, shelters. Through Hana Town, and around south flank of Kau'iki Head (cinder cone) is

a red cinder beach. No facilities. Swimming, snorkeling, excellent sunrises.

Hanaka'ō'ō Beach Park

About 3 miles north of Lahaina on Hwy. 30. Picnicking (tables), swimming. Restrooms, grills. Wheelchair-accessible area, parking, restrooms.

Honokōwai Beach Park

About 5 miles north of Lahaina on Hwy. 30. Picnicking (tables). Restrooms, grills.

Ho'okipa Beach Park

About 7 miles east of Kahului airport on Hwy. 360. Windward shore. Tent camping, picnicking (tables), surfing, boardsailing. Restrooms, grills, shelters. Wheelchair-accessible area and restrooms.

Kalama Beach Park

About 4 miles south of Kīhei on Kīhei Rd. Picnicking (tables), swimming. Restrooms, grills, shelters. Wheelchair-accessible area.

Kalepolepo Beach Park

About 2 miles south of Kīhei on Kīhei Rd. Picnicking (tables). Restrooms.

Kama'ole Beach Park

About 5 miles south of Kīhei on Kīhei Rd. In three sections. Picnicking (tables). Restrooms, grills. Wheelchair-accessible area and restrooms.

Kanaha Beach Park

About 1 mile north of Kahului airport off Hwy. 380. Picnicking (tables), swimming. Restrooms, grills. Wheelchair-accessible area and restrooms.

Kepaniwai Park

About 3 miles west of Wailuku on Hwy. 320. Heritage gardens, stream. Picnicking (tables), swimming (pool), scenic viewing. Restrooms, grills, shelters. Wheelchair-accessible area and restrooms.

Maipoina 'Oe Ia'u Beach Park

About 1 mile south of Kīhei on Kīhei Rd. Picnicking (tables), swimming. Restrooms, grills, shelters.

Paunau Park

About 2 miles south of Lahaina on Hwy. 30. Playground and tot lot. No drinking water.

Rainbow County Park

About 7 miles east of Kahului airport via Hwys. 36 and 390. Camping (fee, very isolated), picnicking. Pavilion, restrooms.

Wai'ehu Beach Park

About 3 miles north of Kahului off Hwy. 340 at Wai'ehu. Picnicking. Restrooms, grills, shelters.

Waihe'e Beach Park

About 5 miles north of Kahului off Hwy. 340 at Waihe'e. Picnicking (tables). Restrooms, grills.

OTHER PARKLANDS

Kaho'olawe

Visible from Maui, this island has been a U.S. Navy bombing and target range since the 1940s. Contains some archaeological sites but is currently off limits. On rare occasions U.S. Navy issues permission to visit.

Molokini

Between Maui and Kaho'olawe, access by boat only. Commercial day-trips out of Kihei and Lahaina. Marine life conservation district and seabird sanctuary. Snorkeling, scuba diving.

The Nature Conservancy's Waikamoi Preserve

P.O. Box 1716
Makawao, HI 96768
(808) 572-7849

Public hikes normally begin at Haleakalā National Park's Hosmer Grove campground, about 37 miles (2 hrs.) southeast of Kahului, via Hwys. 377 and 378. 5,230 acres. Managed by The Nature Conservancy; owned by Haleakalā Ranch Co. Rain forest with rare birds (po'ouli, 'akepeu'ie, Maui parrotbill, yellow-green Maui creeper, crested honey creeper). Camping (limited during hunting periods, permit required), rugged hiking (steep slopes, permit required), goat and pig hunting (permit required), nature study, photography. No pets allowed.

ISLAND OF LĀNA'I

COUNTY PARKLANDS

Dole Park

In Lāna'i City, on Lāna'i Ave. between Seventh and Eighth Sts. Picnicking. Restrooms.

OTHER PARKLANDS

Ko'ele Company

P.O. Box L
Lāna'i City, HI 96763
(808) 565-6661

Camping (fee, permit required). Grills, picnic tables, restrooms. Contact office for information on locations.

ISLAND OF MOLOKA'I

FEDERAL PARKLANDS

Kakahai'a National Wildlife Refuge

c/o Hawaiian and Pacific Islands NWRs
P.O. Box 50167 or 300 Ala Moana Blvd.
Honolulu, HI 96850
(808) 541-1201

5 miles east of Kaunakakai along Hwy. 450. 40 acres. Limited access; contact refuge manager. Pond, marsh. Endangered Hawaiian coot and stilt. Observation, photography.

Kalaupapa National Historical Park

Kalaupapa, Moloka'i, HI 96742

5 miles north of Kualapu'u on Hwy. 470 to overlook and trail down to Makanalua Peninsula at center of the northern coast. 10,726 acres. Access by foot, mule, or airplane. Permit required. Site of colony begun in 1866 for people with Hansen's disease (leprosy). Historical sites. Geological and archaeological features. No camping, restaurants, or stores. Escorted tours available (fee).

STATE PARKLANDS

Division of State Parks, Maui District
P.O. Box 1049 or 54 High St.
Wailuku, HI 96793
(808) 244-4354
Permit required for camping.

Pālā'au State Park

P.O. Box 526
Kaunakakai, HI 96793
(808) 244-4354

3 miles northeast of Kualapu'u off Hwy. 470. 234 forested acres. Scenic overlook of Kalaupapa National Historical Park. Phallic stone. Camping, hiking, picnicking.

COUNTY PARKLANDS

Maui County Dept. of Parks and Recreation
P.O. Box 526
Kaunakakai, HI 96748
(808) 553-3221
Permit required for camping.

Eastend Community Center

At 'Ualapu'e, 21 miles east of airport on Kamehameha Hwy. (Hwy. 450). Picnicking. Athletic field, kitchen, pavilion, restrooms. May be reserved for exclusive use (fee, permit required).

Hālawa Park

At Hālawa, 37 miles east of airport at end of Kamehameha Hwy. (Hwy. 450). Site of early Hawaiian settlement. Hiking trail up to either of two waterfalls, Moa'ula (250 ft.) and Hipuapua (500 ft.), passes through many agricultural terraces and house sites. Large plunge pool at the base of each falls suitable for wading and swimming. Fishing. Restrooms.

Ho'olehua Community Center

At Ho'olehua, 7 miles north of airport via Hwy. 480. Athletic field, kitchen, pavilion, restrooms. May be reserved for exclusive use (fee, permit required).

Kakahai'a Park

At Kawela, 14 miles southeast of airport on Hwy. 450. Picnicking.

Maunaloa Community Center

At Maunaloa, 16 miles west of Kaunakakai on Hwy. 460. Athletic field, kitchen, pavilion, restrooms. May be reserved for exclusive use (fee, permit required).

Mitchell Pauole Center

In Kaunakakai, 9 miles east of airport on Hwy. 460. Swimming. Athletic field, kitchen, pavilion, restrooms, tennis court. May be reserved for exclusive use (fee, permit required).

'O'ne Ali'i Beach Parks 1 and 2

At 'O'ne Ali'i, 12 miles southeast of airport on Hwy. 450. Camping (fee), jogging, picnicking, swimming, fishing. Restrooms, showers, athletic field, pavilion. May be reserved for exclusive use (fee, permit required).

Pāpōhaku Beach Park

At Kalua Koi, 13 miles west of airport. Camping (fee), fishing, picnicking, swimming. Restrooms, showers. May be reserved for exclusive use (fee, permit required).

Pu'u Hauole Mini Park

At Manila Camp, about 9 miles southeast of airport on Hwy. 460. Picnicking. No restrooms.

OTHER PARKLANDS

The Nature Conservancy's Kamakou Preserve

P.O. Box 40
Kualapu'u, HI 96757
(808) 567-6680

About 45 minutes east of Hwy. 46 via Forest Reserve jeep road (about 0.5 mile south of junction of Hwys. 46 and 47) to entrance at Waikolu Lookout; 4-wheel drive needed. 2,774 acres. Managed by The Nature Conservancy; owned by Moloka'i Ranch. 219 uniquely Hawaiian plants; rare birds ('olomao, kakawahie, 'i'iwi, 'amakihi). Registration required for entry; advance notice required for large groups. Camping (at Waikolu Lookout; contact Maui District Forester, Box 1015, Wailuku, HI 96793), hiking (trails), hunting (pigs, goats, axis deer, game birds; registration required), scenic viewing (roads). No pets allowed.

Moloka'i Ranch

P.O. Box 8

Maunaloa, HI 96770
(808) 552-2767

17 miles west of Kaunakakai via Hwy. 460. 59,724 acres. Open to public. Access on unpaved roads by car when dry; 4-wheel-drive when wet. Sandy and rocky beaches. Camping (fee), fishing, crabbing. Limited running water. Entrance fee.

Moloka'i Ranch Wildlife Park

c/o Kalua Koi Hotel
P.O. Box 1977
Maunaloa, HI 96770
(808) 552-2622

3 miles northwest of Maunaloa off Hwy. 460, adjacent to Kalua Koi resort. 1,000 acres with giraffes, axis deer, Indian antelope (blackbuck), barbary sheep (aoudad), eland, kudu, oryx, Rio Grande turkey, rhea birds. 4 tours daily. Fee.

ISLAND OF O'AHU

FEDERAL PARKLANDS

James C. Campbell National Wildlife Refuge

c/o Hawaiian and Pacific Islands NWRs
P.O. Box 50167 or 300 Ala Moana Blvd.
Honolulu, HI 96850
(808) 541-1201

Near Kahuku on northeastern shore. 142 acres. Limited access; contact refuge manager. Spring-fed marsh, man-made ponds. Endangered Hawaiian gallinule, Hawaiian coot, Hawaiian stilt, kōloa (Hawaiian duck), black-crowned night heron. Observation, photography.

Pearl Harbor National Wildlife Refuge

c/o Hawaiian and Pacific Islands NWRs
P.O. Box 50167 or 300 Ala Moana Blvd.
Honolulu, HI 96850
(808) 541-1201

About 10 miles west of Honolulu, within Pearl Harbor Naval Base. 61 acres. Limited access; contact refuge manager. Man-made wetlands. Endangered Hawaiian gallinule, Hawaiian coot, Hawaiian stilt, kōloa (Hawaiian duck), black-crowned night heron. Observation, photography from boundaries.

U.S.S. Arizona Memorial

No. 1 Arizona Memorial Place
Honolulu, HI 96818
(808) 422-0561

About 2 miles west of Honolulu airport off Hwy. 99. Sunken battleship, memorial to those killed in 1941 Japanese attack on Pearl Harbor. Boat tour programs; ticket required. (Tickets are free—first come, first served.)

STATE PARKLANDS

Division of State Parks, O'ahu District
P.O. Box 621 or 1151 Punchbowl St.
Honolulu, O'ahu, HI 96809
(808) 548-7455
Permit required for camping.

'Aina Moana (Magic Island) State Recreation Area

In Honolulu at east (Waikiki) end of Ala Moana Beach Park off Ala Moana (Hwy. 92). 42.7 acres. South shore, seasonal high surf. Picnicking, sand-beach activities, snorkeling, surfing (board, body, wind), swimming.

Diamond Head State Monument

In Honolulu off Diamond Head Road between Makapu'u and 18th aves. 475 acres. Hiking, picnicking. From parking area near restrooms, a trail leads up through World War II battlements to the 760-ft. summit for excellent view of Honolulu, Waikiki, and Koko Head.

Hanauma Bay State Underwater Park

At Hanauma Bay Beach Park, 0.3 mile east of Hawai'i Kai off Kalaniana'ole Hwy. (Hwy. 72). 101 acres. South shore. Scuba diving, snorkeling, swimming. Restrooms, snack bar, telephones, equipment rental at adjacent Hanauma Bay Beach Park. Steep access road with periodic shuttle service (fee).

He'eia State Park

46-465 Kamehameha Hwy. (Hwy. 836) at Kealohi Point, He'eia. 18.4 acres. Good views of Kāne'ohe Bay and He'eia Fishpond. Picnicking. Pavilion, restrooms, night security.

Honolulu Stadium (old site) State Recreation Area

2237 South King St., Honolulu. 9.2 acres. Landscaped community park. Picnicking, jogging, strolling. Parking and restrooms.

'Iolani Palace State Monument

Downtown Honolulu at the corner of South King and Richards sts. 11 acres. National historic landmark. Picnicking. Guided tours of the palace itself are scheduled by the Friends of 'Iolani Palace, (808) 538-1471 (fee). Gift shop, Archives of Hawai'i and Library of Hawai'i Main Branch adjoin.

Ka'ena Point State Park

At end of Farrington Hwy. (Hwy. 930) past Mākua. 853 acres. Leeward shore, seasonal high surf. Wild coastline, sandy beach, large sea cave, hot and dry with little shade. Fishing, hiking, picnicking, porpoise viewing, snorkeling, expert board and bodysurfing, swimming only when calm. Phone, restrooms.

Kahana Valley State Park

55-222 Kamehameha Hwy. (Hwy. 83), at Kahana. 5,220.3 acres. Open only during daylight. Wildland valley. Fruit picking, picnicking, viewing of Huilua Fish Pond. Hiking and pig hunting by permit. Swimming at adjacent beach park.

Kaiaka State Recreation Area

66-449 Hale'iwa Road, just northeast of Hale'iwa Elementary School, off Kamehameha Hwy. (Hwy. 83), or Waialua Beach Rd., Hale'iwa. 52.8 acres. North shore, seasonal high surf. Landscaped coastal park. Fishing, picnicking, snorkeling, swimming. Phone, restrooms.

Kaka'ako Waterfront (Point Panic) State Recreation Area

In Honolulu, at end of Ahui St. off Ala Moana Rd. (Hwy. 92). South shore, seasonal high surf, no shade. Expert surfing, pole fishing. Restrooms.

Kea'iwa Heiau State Recreation Area

At end of 'Aiea Heights Dr., 'Aiea. 384.5 acres. Forest. Camping, hardy hiking, picnicking. Rustic facilities.

Mālaekahana State Recreation Area

Off Kamehameha Hwy. (Hwy. 83), Mālaekahana Beach: Kalanai Beach section 0.6 mile north of Lā'ie; Kahuku section 1.3 miles north of Lā'ie. 110 acres. Windward shore, seasonal high surf. Wooded beach park. Camping (permit required), fishing, picnicking, snorkeling, surfing, swimming. Phone, restrooms, night security. Camping fee and cabins at Kahuku.

Nu'uanu Pali State Wayside

7 miles from Honolulu off Pali Hwy. (Hwy. 61). 5 acres. Scenic lookout of windward O'ahu.

Pu'u o Mahuka Heiau State Monument

Off Pūpūkea Homestead Rd. (Hwy. 835) from Kamehameha Hwy. (Hwy. 83) across from Pūpūkea fire station. 4 acres. Viewing of O'ahu's largest heiau, a national historic landmark.

Pu'u Ualaka'a State Wayside

About 3 miles up Round Top Dr. from Makiki St. in Honolulu. 50 acres. Panoramic view of Honolulu. Hardy family hiking, picnicking in adjacent forest reserve.

Royal Mausoleum State Monument

2261 Nu'uanu Ave., Honolulu. 10 acres. Burial place of Hawaiian royalty. Information service, guided tours by reservation. Picnicking prohibited.

Sacred Falls State Park

2 miles southwest of Hau'ula by trail off Kamehameha Hwy. (Hwy. 83). 1,374.2 acres. Hardy family hiking, closed during rain.

Sand Island State Recreation Area

At end of Sand Island access road, off Nimitz Hwy. (Hwy. 92) in Honolulu. 140 acres. South shore, seasonal high surf. Landscaped coastal park, small sand beach. Camping (permit required), fishing, picnicking, surfing, walking. Boat ramp, pavilion, phone, restrooms, night security. Wheelchair accessible area, restrooms, phones.

Sans Souci State Recreation Area

On Kalākaua Ave. between Kaimana Beach Hotel and War Memorial Natatorium in Waikiki. 1 acre. South shore beach popular for children due to relatively calm and shallow waters. Fishing (regulated), picnicking, board surfing, snorkeling, swimming. Lifeguard, phone. Wheelchair accessible. In 1988 an underwater marine park was designated next to Sans Souci from the War Memorial Natatorium to the Kapahulu Ave. Groin, near the Honolulu Zoo. No fishing allowed. Viewing of reef and near-shore marine life, snorkeling, scuba diving.

Ulu Pō Heiau State Monument

Off Kailua Rd. (Hwy. 61) 0.4 mile northeast of Castle Hospital in Kailua. 8.3 acres. Viewing of heiau ruins and Kawainui marsh.

Wa'ahila Ridge State Recreation Area

At end of Ruth Pl., via Peter St. from St. Louis Dr. off Wai'alae Ave. in St. Louis Heights, Honolulu. 49.9 acres. Norfolk Island pine forest. Hardy family hiking, picnicking.

Wahiawā Freshwater State Recreation Area

380 Walker Ave., off Kamehameha Hwy. (Hwy. 80) just north of Wahiawā Bridge in Wahiawā. 66 acres. Restricted freshwater fishing, picnicking. Boat ramp only for fishing. No swimming or water skiing.

Waimānalo Bay State Recreation Area

20 miles northeast of Honolulu airport via Pali Hwy. (Hwy. 61), Kalaniana'ole Hwy. (Hwy. 72), and Aloiloi St., next to Bellows Air Force Base. 74.8 acres. Large sandy beach, windward shore, seasonal high surf. Picnicking, novice board surfing and bodysurfing, swimming. Phone, restrooms, night security.

Washington Place State Monument

On Beretania St. opposite the State Capitol in Honolulu. 3.1 acres. Hawai'i's oldest continuously occupied residence. Home of the Governor of Hawai'i. Viewing from sidewalk.

Wildlife Sanctuaries

Located on several islands and islets offshore. Landing requirements vary. Contact Hawai'i Div. of Forestry and Wildlife (808) 548-2861 for information.

COUNTY PARKLANDS

Honolulu City & County Dept. of Parks & Recreation
650 S. King St.
Honolulu, HI 96813
(808) 523-4525
Permit required for camping.

Ala Moana Beach Park

In Honolulu, off Ala Moana (Hwy. 92) between Kamakee St. and Atkinson Dr. South shore, sand and reef beach. 32 acres. Picnicking; good swimming, surfing. Bowling green, food, lifeguard, pavilion, phones, restrooms, showers, softball fields, tennis courts. Wheelchair-accessible area, parking, restrooms.

'Aukai Beach Park

35 miles north of Honolulu airport, off Kamehameha Hwy. (Hwy. 83), near Hau'ula. Windward shore. Fair swimming. No facilities.

Barbers Point Beach Park

20 miles west of Honolulu airport via H-1 and Hwy. 95 to end of Olai Rd. Leeward shore, seasonal high surf. Fair fishing,

picnicking, surfing, swimming; good scuba. Phone, restrooms.

Bellows Beach Park

20 miles northeast of Honolulu airport via Pali Hwy. (Hwy. 61) and Kalaniana'ole Hwy. (Hwy. 72), near Bellows Air Force Base. Windward-shore sand beach, seasonal high surf. Trailer and tent camping (weekends and holidays), picnicking, fair beginners' surfing, good bodysurfing, paipo surfing, swimming. Lifeguard (summers and weekends only), phone, restrooms, showers. Wheelchair-accessible area, restrooms.

Blaisdell Park

In Honolulu, about 0.5 mile east of Pearl City off Hwy. 99. South shore. Picnicking. Phone, restrooms.

Chun's Reef—Kawailoa

About 28 miles north of Honolulu airport off Hwy. 83 at Kawailoa Beach. North shore, surfing contest site. Fair swimming; good fishing, snorkeling, swimming. Phone. No facilities.

Diamond Head Beach Park

Across from Diamond Head State Monument on Diamond Head Rd. South shore. Moderate scuba diving, fair surfing and boardsailing (exposed coral), poor swimming. Phone. No facilities.

'Ehukai Beach Park

About 7 miles north of Hale'iwa off Hwy. 83. North shore, sand and reef beach, seasonal high surf. Surfing contest and "Banzai Pipeline" site. Picnicking; expert surfing (currents, reef); good snorkeling, swimming when surf is flat. Lifeguard, phone, restrooms, showers.

'Ewa Beach Park (Pu'uloa)

About 4 miles southeast of 'Ewa off Hwy. 76. South shore, seasonal high surf. Picnicking, fair swimming, good beginners' surf. Phone, restrooms, basketball and volleyball courts, softball field, children's play apparatus.

Fort Derussy

The west end of Waikiki off Kalakaua Ave. and Ala Moana. South shore. Picnicking, snorkeling, surfing, swimming. Lifeguard, phone, restrooms.

Hale'iwa Ali'i Beach Park

About 25 miles north of Honolulu airport off Hwy. 821 near Hale'iwa. North shore reef beach, seasonal high surf. John Kalili Surf Center, surfing contest site. Picnicking, good scuba diving,

fair snorkeling, excellent surfing for beginners when low surf (dangerous currents when high), swimming. Lifeguard, phone, restrooms, showers.

Hale'iwa Beach Park

About 25 miles north of Honolulu airport off Hwy. 83 near Hale'iwa. Trailer and tent camping, picnicking; fair snorkeling, surfing, boardsailng, swimming (coral). Baseball and softball fields, basketball and volleyball courts, food, pavilion, phone, restrooms. Wheelchair-accessible area, restrooms.

Hanauma Bay Beach Park

10 miles east of Waikiki off Hwy. 72. South shore reef beach, seasonal high surf. Marine life conservation district. Picnicking; good scuba diving, snorkeling, swimming. Food, lifeguard, pavilion, phone, restrooms, showers. Wheelchair-accessible area, parking, restrooms.

Hau'ula Beach Park

About 35 miles north of Honolulu airport off Hwy. 83 near Hau'ula. Windward shore, seasonal high surf. Trailer and tent camping, good fishing, picnicking, fair snorkeling, poor swimming. Pavilion, phone, restrooms.

Hawaiian Electric ("Tracks") Beach Park

About 18 miles west of Honolulu airport off Hwy. 93. Leeward shore, seasonal high surf. Picnicking, bodysurfing, surfing. No facilities.

Ho'omaluhia Park

About 10 miles east of Honolulu off Likelike Hwy. (Hwy. 63) at Kāne'ohe. 400 acres. Constructed as part of a flood control project for urban Windward O'ahu. Picnicking, camping by permit, community center and gallery. Walking trails.

Ka'a'awa Beach Park

About 22 miles north of Honolulu airport off Hwy. 83 near Ka'a'awa. Windward shore. Camping, picnicking; good snorkeling, swimming. Phone, restrooms. Wheelchair-accessible area, restrooms.

Kahana Bay Beach Park

About 25 miles north of Honolulu airport off Hwy. 83 near Kahana. Windward shore. Trailer camping, picnicking; good boating, fishing, swimming; fair beginner's surfing. Phone, restrooms. Wheelchair-accessible area, restrooms.

Kahe Point Beach Park

About 14 miles west of Honolulu airport off Hwy. 93. Leeward shore, seasonal high surf. Trailer and tent camping, picnicking; good fishing, scuba diving, snorkeling; good surfing, swimming nearby. Phone, restrooms.

Kailua Beach Park

At Kailua, 25 miles from Waikiki Beach on Hwy. 72. Windward shore, seasonal high surf, regatta site. Picnicking; good boating, sailing, snorkeling, bodysurfing, boardsailing, swimming. Boat ramp, food, lifeguard, pavilion, phone, restrooms, showers. Wheelchair-accessible area, restrooms.

Kaiona Beach Park

25 miles northeast of Honolulu airport via Pali Hwy. (Hwy. 61) and Kalaniana'ole Hwy. (Hwy. 72). Windward shore. Picnicking; fair fishing, snorkeling, swimming. Boat ramp, phone, restrooms.

Kalae-oio Beach Park

About 22 miles north of Honolulu airport off Hwy. 83 near Ka'a'awa. Windward shore, seasonal high surf. Picnicking, snorkeling, poor swimming. Phone.

Kāne'ohe Beach Park

15 miles northeast of Honolulu airport via Likelike Hwy. (Hwy. 63) and Hwy. 65. Windward shore. Picnicking, poor swimming (mudflats). Restrooms.

Kapi'olani Park

In Honolulu, at end of Kalākaua Ave. between Waikiki Beach and Diamond Head. 300 acres. South shore. Picnicking, fair snorkeling, surfing, swimming. Aquarium, archery field, food, gardens, golf driving range, lifeguard, natatorium, phone, polo field, restrooms, tennis courts, zoo. Honolulu Zoo features habitat exhibits for Hawaiian birds and a flock of tame nēnē (fee). War Memorial Natatorium is no longer useable. Waikiki Aquarium (University of Hawai'i) features exhibits on Hawaiian marine life, occasional programs open to the public, and a gift shop. The Waikiki Shell and adjacent Kodak Hula Show are additional attractions. Wheelchair-accessible area, limited parking, restrooms.

Kaupo Beach Park

About 25 miles east of Honolulu airport via Pali Hwy. (Hwy. 61) and Hwy. 72. Windward shore, seasonal high surf. Good fishing, snorkeling, beginner's board surfing, swimming. No facilities.

Kea'au Beach Park

About 3 miles north of Wai'anae off Hwy. 93. Leeward shore, seasonal high surf. Trailer and tent camping, picnicking; good fishing, skin diving, snorkeling, body and paipo surfing, swimming. Phone, restrooms.

Ke'ehi Lagoon Beach Park

About 4 miles east of Honolulu airport off Hwy. 64. South shore. Picnicking; good sailing, water skiing; poor swimming. Pavilion, phone, restrooms, tennis courts, rugby-baseball-softball fields.

Koko Head Beach Park

About 13 miles east of Waikiki on Hwy. 72. 1,200 acres. South-shore sandy beach. Picnicking; good scuba diving, body and paipo surfing; swimming (currents). Botanic garden, food, lifeguard, phone, restrooms.

Kualoa Point Park

22 miles north of Honolulu airport off Hwy. 83. Windward shore, sand and reef beach. Camping, picnicking, snorkeling, swimming. Lifeguard (summers and weekends only), phone, restrooms, night security, showers.

Kūhiō Beach Park

In Honolulu, between Waikiki and Diamond Head on Kalakaua Ave. South shore, seasonal high surf. Picnicking; good swimming, bodysurfing, paipo surfing, swimming. Food, lifeguard, phone, restrooms. Wheelchair-accessible area, restrooms, phone.

Kuilei Cliffs Beach Park

2 miles east of Waikiki on Diamond Head Rd. South shore, seasonal high surf. Picnicking, snorkeling, surfing, swimming. Phone.

Kuli'ou'ou Beach Park

About 8 miles east of Waikiki off Hwy. 72. South shore. Picnicking, poor swimming (mudflats). Basketball courts, children's play apparatus. Phone, restrooms.

Laenani Beach Park

17 miles north of Honolulu airport via Likelike Hwy. (Hwy. 63) and Kahekile Hwy., at Kahalu'u. Picnicking, poor swimming. Baseball and volleyball courts, softball field, children's play apparatus, phone, restrooms.

Lā'ie Beach Park

38 miles north of Waikiki off Hwy. 83 at Lā'ie. Windward shore, seasonal high surf. Excellent bodysurfing, fair swimming. Phone.

Laniakea Beach—Kawailoa

3 miles north of Hale'iwa off Hwy. 83. Good fishing, snorkeling, surfing; fair swimming. Phone.

Lualualei Beach Park

0.5 mile south of Wai'anae on Hwy. 93. Leeward shore, seasonal high surf. Camping, picnicking, good fishing, poor swimming (coral). Phone, restrooms.

Mā'ili Beach Park

1.5 miles south of Wai'anae on Hwy. 93. Leeward shore, seasonal high surf. Sand and reef beach. Picnicking; good fishing, skin diving, snorkeling, surfing, swimming. Lifeguard, phones, restrooms, showers.

Mākaha Beach Park

About 3 miles north of Wai'anae on Hwy. 93. Leeward shore, sand and reef beach, seasonal high surf. Camping, picnicking; good fishing, skin diving, snorkeling; top surfing for experts; fair swimming. Lifeguard, phone, restrooms, showers. Wheelchair-accessible area, restrooms.

Makapu'u Beach Park

15 miles northeast of Waikiki on Hwy. 72. Windward shore, sand and reef, seasonal high surf. Surfing contest site. Summer camping, picnicking, snorkeling, excellent body and paipo surfing, poor swimming (currents). Lifeguard, phone, restrooms, showers.

Mākua Beach

About 9 miles north of Wai'anae on Hwy. 93. Leeward shore. Good fishing, skin diving, snorkeling, swimming; very good scuba; expert surfing (rocks). Phone.

Mauna Lahilahi Beach Park

1 mile north of Wai'anae on Hwy. 93. Leeward shore, seasonal high surf. Picnicking; good fishing, skin diving, snorkeling; fair swimming. Phone, restrooms.

Maunalua Bay Beach Park

About 8 miles east of Waikiki off Hwy. 72. South shore. Picnicking; good boating, fishing, snorkeling; fair boardsailing, poor swimming. Restrooms, phone.

Mokulē'ia Beach Park

About 8 miles west of Hale'iwa on Hwy. 930. Leeward shore, seasonal high surf. Trailer and tent camping, picnicking; good snorkeling, skin diving and fishing; poor swimming (coral), fair surfing (reefs and currents). Phone, restrooms.

Nānākuli Beach Park

About 6 miles south of Wai'anae on Hwy. 93. Leeward shore, sand beach, seasonal high surf. Trailer and tent camping, picnicking; good fishing, snorkeling, surfing, swimming (exposed reefs); fair scuba diving. Lifeguard (summers, weekends only), phones, restrooms, showers.

One'ula Beach Park (Hau Bush)

About 5 miles southwest of 'Ewa off Hwy. 76. South shore. Fair fishing, picnicking, surfing, swimming, and restrooms.

Pearl Harbor Park

National historic landmark. Picnicking, good crabbing, fishing. Restrooms. Wheelchair-accessible area, restrooms.

Pōka'ī Bay Beach Park

At Wai'anae, 21 miles west of Pearl City on Hwy. 93. Leeward shore, sand and reef beach. Excavated but unrestored heiau. Several local canoe clubs build, repair, and sail traditional Hawaiian outrigger canoes here. Picnicking; excellent boating, fishing, sailing, snorkeling, swimming; moderate scuba diving in selected areas; fair surfing nearby. Lifeguard, phone, restrooms, showers.

Punalu'u Beach Park

About 6 miles south of Lā'ie on Hwy. 83. Windward shore. Trailer and tent camping, picnicking; good fishing, snorkeling, swimming. Phone, restrooms.

Pūpūkea Beach Park

5 miles north of Hale'iwa on Hwy. 83. North shore, seasonal high surf. Marine life conservation district. Picnicking, boardsailing, good snorkeling and restricted fishing when calm, poor swimming. Basketball and volleyball courts, children's play apparatus, phone, recreation building, restrooms.

Queen's Surf Beach Park

In Honolulu, across from Kapi'olani Park off Kalākaua Ave. South shore. Picnicking; good surfing, swimming. Food, lifeguard, pavilion, restrooms. Wheelchair-accessible area, restrooms, phones.

Sandy Beach Park

14 miles east of Waikiki on Hwy. 72. South shore, sand and reef, seasonal high surf. Surfing, expert bodysurfing, swimming. Lifeguard, restrooms, showers, phone. Wheelchair accessible.

Sunset Beach

7 miles west of Lā'ie on Hwy. 83. North shore, sand and reef beach, seasonal high surf. Surfing contest site. Picnicking; expert surfing (currents); good fishing; snorkeling, swimming when calm. Lifeguard, phone.

Swanzy Beach Park

8 miles south of Lā'ie on Hwy. 83. Windward shore. Trailer and tent camping, picnicking, fishing, snorkeling, poor swimming (exposed coral). Basketball and volleyball courts, softball field, children's play apparatus, lifeguard, phone, restrooms.

Ulehawa Beach Park

3 miles south of Wai'anae on Hwy. 93. Leeward shore, seasonal high surf. Picnicking; good fishing, skin diving, snorkeling, surfing, swimming. Phones, restrooms.

Waiāhole Beach Park

20 miles northeast of Honolulu airport via Likelike Hwy. (Hwy. 63) to Kamehameha Hwy. (Hwy. 83), at Waiāhole. Poor swimming (mudflats). No facilities.

Wai'alae Beach Park

15 miles east of Honolulu airport off Kalaniana'ole Hwy. (Hwy. 72). South shore. Picnicking; good fishing; fair snorkeling, surfing; poor swimming. Phone, restrooms.

Waiale'e Beach

6 miles west of Lā'ie on Hwy. 83. North shore, seasonal high surf. Snorkeling; expert surfing (dangerous rocks); swimming. Phone.

Wai'anae Regional Park

0.5 mile north of Wai'anae on Hwy. 93. Leeward shore. Picnicking, snorkeling. Tennis courts, softball field, phone, restrooms.

Waikiki Beach Center

In Waikiki, off Kalākaua Ave. South shore, sand and reef. Canoeing, picnicking, good swimming, surfing. Food, lifeguard, lockers, phone, restrooms, showers, surfboard rentals. Wheelchair-accessible area, restrooms, phones.

Wailupe Beach Park

18 miles northeast of Honolulu airport off Kalaniana'ole Hwy. (Hwy. 72). South shore. Picnicking, poor swimming. Phone, restrooms.

Waimānalo Beach Park

22 miles northeast of Honolulu airport via Pali Hwy. (Hwy. 61) and Kalaniana'ole Hwy. (Hwy. 72). Windward shore, seasonal high surf. Trailer and tent camping, picnicking; excellent sailing, snorkeling, swimming, expert surfing. Baseball and softball fields, basketball and volleyball courts, pavilion, phone, restrooms. Wheelchair-accessible area, restrooms.

Waimea Bay Beach Park

13 miles west of Lā'ie on Hwy. 83. North shore, sand and reef beach, seasonal high surf. Picnicking, expert surfing and bodysurfing (currents); good snorkeling and swimming when calm. Lifeguard, phone, restrooms, showers. Wheelchair-accessible area, restrooms.

OTHER PARKLANDS

Kāneakē Heiau Park

c/o Sheraton Mākaha Resort
P.O. Box 900 or 84-626 Mākaha Valley Rd.
Wai'anae, HI 96792
(808) 695-9511

About 5 miles north of Wai'anae at end of Mākaha Valley Rd. off Hwy. 93. One of Hawai'i's best preserved religious temples, built during 14th century. Owned by Honolulu Federal Savings & Loan. Accessibility depends on weather and owner's approval; inquire at hotel. Shuttle service by reservation for hotel guests. No facilities.

Moanalua Gardens Foundation

Kamananui Valley 1352 Pineapple Place
Honolulu, HI 96819
(808) 839-5334

Located near the airport and Tripler Army Hospital, on the outskirts of urban Honolulu, this public park, privately owned and managed, offers a wide range of walks, treks, hikes, and cultural experiences, displays, and presentations year-round. Parking, access via TheBus Transit, restrooms, gift shop.

Paradise Park

3737 Manoa Rd.
Honolulu, HI 96822
(808) 988-2141, 988-6686

Conceived and built as a tourist attraction utilizing imported, colorful birds. Restaurant, gift shop, tours, trained bird shows in lush, tropical setting (fee). Parking.

Sea Life Park

Makapu'u Point
Waimānalo, HI 96795
(808) 259-7933

Public portion of a research and animal behavior training complex. Hawaiian reef tank exhibit of marine life in its natural habitat, trained dolphin and whale programs. Admission fee includes all exhibits and programs. A separate gift shop and food area does not require admission. Parking, restrooms, food, wheelchair access, open daily.

U.S.S. Bowfin *Pacific Fleet Submarine*

Memorial Association
11 Arizona Memorial Dr.
Honolulu, HI 96818
(808) 423-1341

About 2 miles west of Honolulu airport off Hwy. 99, adjacent to U.S.S. *Arizona* Memorial Visitor Center. 3.77 acres. WWII diesel-electric submarine, sank 44 enemy vessels. Self-guided tour of topside and below deck (fee). Museum with gift shop.

Waimea Falls Park

59-864 Kamehameha Hwy.
Hale'iwa, HI
(808) 638-8511 or 932-1531

About 15 miles west of Lā'ie off Hwy. 83. 1,800 acres. Visitor center, arboretum, botanical garden, wildlife, diving shows, Hawaiian games demonstrations, narrated minibus rides through botanical, archaeological, and geological features. Swimming and picnicking at the falls are permitted. The only interpreted archaeological sites on O'ahu are here—sometimes by guides, otherwise by signs. Entrance fee. (Restaurant, snack bar, and gift shop are outside entrance-fee area.)

ISLAND OF KAUA'I

FEDERAL PARKLANDS

Hanalei National Wildlife Refuge

c/o P.O. Box 87
Kilauea, HI 96754
(808) 541-1201

Visible from overlook 1.5 miles east of Hanalei or 6.5 miles west of Kilauea on Hwy. 56. Observation from vehicles along Ohiki Rd. beginning at the west end of Hanalei River bridge. Entry by special permit from refuge manager. 917 acres. River bottom land, taro farms, wooded slopes. Endangered kōloa (Hawaiian duck), Hawaiian gallinule, Hawaiian coot, Hawaiian stilt.

Hulē'ia National Wildlife Refuge

c/o P.O. Box 87
Kīlauea, HI 96754
(808) 541-1201

Viewing from Menehune (Alakoko) Fish Pond overlook along Hulemalu Rd. out of Nawiliwili, or from Ha'ikū and Ahina rds. off Hulemalu Road west of Puhi Rd. Entry for special projects by written approval from refuge manager. 238 acres seasonally-flooded river bottom, estuary, wooded slopes. Endangered kōloa (largest population), Hawaiian gallinule, Hawaiian coot, Hawaiian stilt.

Kīlauea Point National Wildlife Refuge

c/o P.O. Box 87
Kīlauea, HI 96754
(808) 541-1201

1 mile north of Kīlauea. 167 acres. Cliffs, headlands, Kīlauea Lighthouse. Red-footed boobies, shearwaters, great frigatebirds, brown boobies, red- and white-tailed tropicbirds, Laysan albatrosses. Wildlife observation and study. Hiking trails, parking, gift shop, restrooms.

STATE PARKLANDS

Division of State Parks, Kaua'i District
P.O. Box 1671 or 3060 Eiwa St.
Līhu'e, HI 96766
(808) 245-4444
Permit required for all camping.

Ahukini State Recreation Pier

About 2 miles east of Līhu'e at end of Ahukini Rd. (Hwy. 570). 0.8 acre. Ocean pier fishing. Wheelchair-accessible area.

Hā'ena State Park

40 miles north of Līhu'e on, KūhiōHwy. (Hwy. 56), at Hā'ena. 61.7 acres. Wildland, wet caves. Beach activities, fishing, hiking, scenic viewing.

Kalalau—see Nā Pali Coast State Park

Kōke'e State Park

15 miles north of Kekaha on Kōke'e Rd. (Hwy. 550). Adjoins Waimea Canyon State Park. 4,345 acres. Wildland, rain forest, canyon. Tent and trailer camping, fishing, hiking, pig hunting, nature study, plum picking, picnicking, scenic viewing. Cabins, pavilion, visitor center, food service. Wheelchair-accessible area and restrooms. Concessionaire: Kōke'e Lodge, P.O. Box 819, Waimea, HI 96796, (808) 335-6061.

Lydgate State Park—see Wailua River State Park

Miloli'i—see Nā Pali Coast State Park

Nā Pali Coast State Park

40 miles north of Līhu'e on Kūhiō Hwy. (Hwy. 56). Accessible by foot (on Kalalau Trail at entrance to Hā'ena State Park) and boat. 6,175 acres. Includes Kalalau, Nu'alolo Kai, Miloli'i areas. Remote wildlands, primitive area. Backpacking, tent camping, hiking, shore fishing, seasonal goat hunting, risky swimming and wading (currents).

Nu'alolo Kai—see Nā Pali Coast State Park

Polihale State Park

5 miles north of Mana via dirt road off Kaumuali'i Hwy. (Hwy. 50). 137.5 acres. Hot, dry area. Tent and trailer camping, bodysurfing, shore fishing, picnicking (shelters), summer swimming, scenic viewing. Grills, pavilion, showers, tables, restrooms. Wheelchair-accessible area and restrooms.

Russian Fort Elizabeth State Historical Park

About 0.5 mile south of Waimea off Kaumuali'i Hwy. (Hwy. 50). 17.3 acres. Boulder-built Russian fort. Self-guided walk. Restrooms.

Wailua River State Park

About 7 miles north of Līhu'e off Kūhiō Hwy. (Hwy. 56). 1,125.9 acres. Includes Lydgate beach area. Lush river valley, riverboat cruise (fee). River and shore fishing, picnicking, scenic viewing, sunbathing, swimming (ocean pool). Food service, gift shop. Lydgate area and pavilion wheelchair accessible; Wailua marina area and restrooms wheelchair accessible.

Waimea Canyon State Park

11.1 miles north of Kekaha on Kōke'e Rd. (Hwy. 550). Adjoins Kōke'e State Park. 1,866.4 acres. Overlooks Waimea Canyon gorge. Seasonal trout fishing, hiking, picnicking, scenic viewing,

pig and seasonal goat hunting nearby. Pavilion. Wheelchair-accessible area.

COUNTY PARKLANDS

Kaua'i County Div. of Parks & Recreation
4280A Rice St., Bldg. B
Līhu'e, HI 96766
(808) 245-8821
Permit (fee) required for camping.

Anahola Beach Park

15 miles north of Līhu'e on Kūhiō Hwy. (Hwy. 56.). 1.54 acres. Swimming. Showers, restroom.

'Anini Beach Park

About 30 miles north of Līhu'e on Kūhiō Hwy. (Hwy. 56.). 2.13 acres. Tent camping, swimming. Grills, pavilion, showers, tables, restrooms.

Hā'ena Beach Park

40 miles north of Līhu'e on Kūhiō Hwy. (Hwy. 56.). 4.72 acres. Tent and trailer camping, unsafe swimming. Grills, pavilion, showers, tables, restrooms.

Hanalei Beach Park

33 miles north of Līhu'e on Kūhiō Hwy. (Hwy. 56.). 2.17 acres. Swimming. Grill, tables, restrooms.

Hanalei Pavilion Park

33 miles north of Līhu'e on Kūhiō Hwy. (Hwy. 56.). 1.34 acres. Unsafe swimming. Grill, pavilion, showers, tables, restroom.

Hanamā'ulu Beach Park

3 miles north of Līhu'e on Kūhiō Hwy. (Hwy. 56.). 6.46 acres. Tent and trailer camping. Grills, pavilion, showers, tables, restrooms. Wheelchair-accessible area.

Hanapēpē Pavilion Park

18 miles southwest of Līhu'e on Kaumuali'i Hwy. (Hwy. 50.). 0.81 acre. Unsafe swimming. Grills, pavilion, tables, tennis courts, restrooms.

Kapa'a Beach Park

10 miles north of Līhu'e on Kūhiō Hwy. (Hwy. 56.). 15.4 acres. Swimming. Grill, pavilion, showers, tables, restroom.

Kekaha Beach Park

27 miles west of Lihu'e on Kaumuali'i Hwy. (Hwy. 50). 30.7 acres. Grills, pavilion, tables, restrooms.

Lucy Wright Park

24 miles west of Lihu'e on Kaumuali'i Hwy. (Hwy. 50) at Waimea. 4.48 acres. Tent camping, surfing, swimming. Restrooms, showers.

Niumalu Beach Park

About 3 miles southeast of Lihu'e, at end of Hwy. 58. 3.41 acres. Tent and trailer camping, swimming. Grills, pavilion, showers, tables, restrooms.

Po'ipū Beach Park

14 miles south of Lihu'e, via Hwy. 520 off Kaumuali'i Hwy. (Hwy 50). 3.86 acres. Surfing. Pavilions, playground, showers, tables, restrooms. Wheelchair-accessible area.

Salt Pond Park

22 miles southwest of Lihu'e, at end of Hwy. 543 off Kaumuali'i Hwy. (Hwy. 50). 5.90 acres. Tent camping, surfing, swimming. Pavilion, showers, restrooms, surfing, swimming. Wheelchair-accessible area.

OTHER PARKLANDS

Kahili Mountain Park

P.O. Box 298
Kōloa, HI 96756
(808) 742-9921

Off Kaumuali'i Hwy. (Hwy. 50) west, 7 miles from Po'ipū Beach, 20 minutes from Lihu'e airport. 215 acres. Owned by Seventh Day Adventist Church. Fishing, hiking, horseback riding. Cabins by reservation (fee).

Olu Pua Botanical Gardens

Kalaheo, HI 96741
(808) 332-8182

Just past Kalaheo on Kaumuali'i Hwy. (Hwy. 50). Originally part of a pineapple manager's estate. Gardens feature commercial and exotic plants, hibiscus, palm trees, flowering shade trees. Self-guided or guided tour available. Entrance fee.

Pacific Tropical Botanical Garden

P.O. Box 340
Lawa'i, 96765
(808) 332-7361

At the end of Hailima Rd. off Hwy. 530. 286 acres. Built from the John Allerton estate, the garden is a research and educational institution and also offers tours. The garden seeks to gather for study, protection, and propagation as many of the world's tropical plants, especially endangered ones, as possible. Entrance fee.

Keeping in touch with the Hawai'i Geographic Series

Falcon Press brings you the talent of America's best outdoor photographers and the knowledge of the best writers in the Hawai'i Geographic Series.

Each book explores a different facet of Hawai'i in magnificent, full-color photos and clear, concise text that will instruct as well as entertain you. Look for future publications examining the state's geology, history, culture, natural resources, recreation, and scenic beauty. All books in the Hawai'i Geographic Series will be similar in format and quality to this book.

For more information on books and calendars published by Falcon Press, write for a free catalog to Falcon Press, P.O. Box 1718, Helena, MT 59624, or call toll-free 1-800-582-BOOK.

▶ *In a steamy climax, pāhoehoe lava from Kīlauea ends its long journey to the ocean.* MICHAEL S. SAMPLE

About the Hawai'i Geographic Society

The Hawai'i Geographic Society had its beginning in 1947 when Laurence and Ethyl Bowen formed the organization in close association with the Kiwanis Club of Honolulu. The original goal was to bring the world to Hawai'i through the regular presentation of travelogue and other 16mm color-film programs to schools and other audiences throughout the islands. This activity continues with the society offering monthly programs on O'ahu and Hawai'i islands.

In 1969 Board Member Richard Conger invited David E. Baker and Willis H. Moore onto the Board of Directors in hopes the society would expand towards bringing information about Hawai'i to the rest of the world. The society investigated publishing a magazine or some other form of informative and colorful presentation, but implementation was postponed.

In 1980 a publications program began modestly with the Pacific Islands Map, followed by other maps relating to Hawai'i and the Pacific Islands. Several pamphlets and a book, *Honolulu: Historic and Sociological Profile of a Unique City,* have also been issued. The Pacific Islands Map, which is updated anually, has passed its one millionth copy.

In 1987 a separate division was established, Hawai'i Geographic Publications, to oversee both publishing endeavors and the operation of an information center and maps and books store in Honolulu.

Hawai'i Geographic Society is an independent, private, not-for-profit, educational Hawai'i corporation and is supported by annual member dues, donations, admissions, and sales.

Willis H. Moore

Maps and books about Hawai'i are available from:
Hawai'i Geographic Maps & Books
P.O. Box 1698
Honolulu, HI 96806-1698
(808) 538-3952